90 DAYS TO REBOOT YOUR CAREER

LAURA MARIANI

ABOUT THE AUTHOR

Laura Mariani is an Author, Speaker and Entrepreneur.

Gabrielle, her latest novel, has been described as *"an incredible novel that combines everything the reader would want and more in a story. It has a bold, moving, and captivating plot that will keep you hooked from start to finish, brilliant world and character building, and of course incredibly addictive".*

Laura is incredibly passionate about helping other women to break through barriers limiting their personal and/or professional fulfillment. Her best selling nonfiction *STOP IT! It is all in your head* and the *THINK, LOOK & ACT THE PART* series have been described as success and transformation 101.

She started her consulting business after a successful career as Senior HR Director within global brands in FMCG, Retail, Media and Pharma.

Laura is a Fellow of the Chartered Institute of Personnel & Development (FCIPD), Fellow of the Australian Human Resources Institute (FAHRI), Fellow of the Institute of Leadership & Management (FInstLM), Member of the Society of Human Resources Management (SHRM) and Member of the Change Institute.

She is based in London, England with a strong penchant for travel and visiting new places.

Laura is a food lover, ballet fanatic, passionate about music, art, theatre. She likes painting and drawing (for self-expression not selling but hey, you never know...), tennis, rugby, and of course fashion (the Pope is Catholic after all).

www.thepeoplealchemist.com

twitter.com/PeopleAlchemist
instagram.com/lauramariani_author
linkedin.com/in/lauramariani-fcipd

CONTENTS

PART I

QUOTE

STOP IT! IT IS ALL IN YOUR HEAD

BLAH BLAH BLAH ...

TELL ME WHAT YOU WANT, WHAT YOU REALLY REALLY WANT

THINK OUTSIDE THE BOX: WHAT BOX?

THE HERO JOURNEY

PART II
90 DAYS TO YOUR NEW CAREER

THINK THE PART

LOOK THE PART

ACT THE PART

ISBN-13: 9781838281298

*To every woman out there waiting
to be perfect before taking action,
for the perfect circumstances
just remember:*

**Perfection is
boring.
Be awesome
instead.
Start today!**

#SmashYourCeiling

WHY THIS BOOK

I love books, and I read like my life depends on them. I believe that books can have the same power as role models: I have used them many times and adopted some *'virtual mentors'* in my never-ending quest for continuous learning and life experimentation.

BOOKS ARE YOUR FRIENDS

I believe that if you need to solve a problem, answer a question, or learn a new skill, there's a good chance you can find what you're looking for in a book. But to make the most of it, you need to digest the books ask them questions. Then make notes, summarize, underline: treat them as an experience—a conversation.

And then, most importantly, apply the lessons learnt in your life — without application, it is just theory. Life is a never-ending journey, with experiments and lessons at every corner and a book to match them.

. . .

The purpose of this book is straightforward; to be a practical and clear, direct-action personal improvement guide, written with the sole objective of helping every woman who reads to achieve what she desires in her career. Your pocket (ok, handbag) coach helping you, nudging you, sometimes shouting at you if you give up or make too many excuses.

It contains techniques and exercises that demonstrate that you do not need to be defeated by anything and have precisely what you want.

Altogether too many women are defeated by everyday circumstances. So they go struggling, perhaps even whining through their days (now, be honest here) with a sense of resentment. I have learned the hard way by trial and error in my career.

I'm not saying to ignore or minimise the hardship and injustices in the world but dominate them. Nevertheless, you can rise above obstacles that ordinarily might defeat you with the right mindset and attitude.

So what is this new book all about?

In practice, this book is an anthology of my previous non-fiction books (STOP IT! It is all in your head plus the Think, Look and Act The Part series) but with a difference. You might say, "It's not a new book", and technically, you are right. However, there are many revised / new content and bonus features.

Let me explain.

The STOP IT! Book was written as a call to action for women to take ownership and responsibility for their career and climb that ladder up to the ceiling and smash it. The book also contained some exercises to help along the way.

The series came next (Think, Look & Act the Part); all workbooks could/can be used both as an accompaniment and complement to the STOP IT! Book and/or as an independent, stand-alone self-discovery self-empowerment journey.

It did require some workarounds from the readers who got them all, like skipping the exercises in STOP IT! and repeating some of the parts in the workbooks. But, on the other hand, for the readers who are only interested in the STOP IT! Book and/or on just one part of the journey (Think, Look or Act), those books are still very beneficial (if I say so myself).

I gather you are not one of those readers, and now everything is together in sequence, in one friendly and tidy place. And with new content.

90 DAYS TO REBOOT YOUR CAREER

Part II of the book is laid out as a journey for 90 consecutive days with new exercises specific to the area tackled (Think, Look or Act) and a bonus.

This part is here to help you and nudge you step-by-step along the way to upgrade your mindset and make winning an essential part of your life and business (Think). Then it shows you how to elevate your brand and present your unique Best Self, a key part of your life and business (Look). And finally, it guides you to act despite fear, with challenges to push your boundaries.

Repetition intentionally creates new daily habits/patterns and more profound self-realization and releases a more powerful self-image.

You see, we are creatures of habit: 95% of our decisions are made without conscious minds. And this happens in a millisecond with our subconscious, driven by routine and automatisms.

Unfortunately, a few days are not sufficient to change your habits. And to free yourself from your old paradigms.

Yes, challenges are good fun. But they are not enough to ingrain what has been learnt into the subconscious so much so that it becomes a belief that runs you. For this, you need routines.

BUILDING NEW HABITS

Twenty-one days is often used as the time it takes to build a new habit. Why is that?

In The 1950s, Maxwell Maltz, a plastic surgeon, noticed a strange pattern among his patients. He saw that the average patient took about 21 days to get used to their new face post-surgery. Ditto, patients with limb amputation. They would sense a phantom limb for about 21 days before adjusting to the unique situation. These experiences led Maltz to think about behavioral changes.

21 OR 66 DAYS?

Maltz went on to say that a <u>minimum</u> of about 21 days is required for an old mental image to dissipate. And a new one to stick. He said so in his best-selling book "Psycho-Cybernetics". But the "minimum of about 21 days" became just 21 days. And there goes the myth.

Psychologist Dr Philippa Lally developed an experiment to find out how long it takes to establish and cement a new habit at University College London. The study showed it takes around 66 days to go from conscious execution to automation.

The brain prefrontal cortex builds like a muscle (the area gets physically more prominent). And then, it is "reprogrammed" with new neuropathways. But after 90 days, the habit becomes a lifestyle.

· · ·

You see, willpower is a limited resource that is depleted by resisting temptations—AND making consistent decisions. Good habits help prevent this; they require no decisions.

Of course, when you start, you require willpower before whatever it is becomes a habit. But once it has taken root, you can take your hands off the wheel and go on autopilot.

Self-discipline is **continuously** choosing to think, say and do what is in your best interest. Success is a habit. And you CAN build habits that run you.

It is time to take ownership and stop blaming other people, society, etc. It is time to be selfish and look after yourself and what you want without guilt. If you are frustrated, annoyed, disillusioned, you will project that into your professional and personal life.

This book will help you to decide:
What YOU want, no one else.
Why YOU REALLY want it.
What YOU need, no one else.
Why YOU need it.
What YOU feel, no one else.

And in these 90 days, I'll steer you in your journey, step by step, day after day and show you how. Woman to Woman.

Time to adopt airlines' guidelines — put your oxygen mask first, and let's fly, baby!

HOW TO USE THIS BOOK

Hello there and welcome!

You have decided to go all in and immerse yourself in this journey, congratulations!!

This book is comprised of sections: PART I : STOP IT! And Part II: 90 Days to Reboot Your Career and Think, Look and Act The Part.

Ideally, you should start by firstly reading Part I: STOP IT! And then proceed to Part II : The 90 Days. However feel free to skip Part I and jump straight into action and revisit STOP IT! at your leisure.

Above all, I'd recommend that you spend real time going through Part II: The 90 Days. Don't use the usual excuse I haven't got the time. 30 minutes a day for yourself can change your life.

If you still insist on saying you haven't got the time, then I can think of three reasons:

1. You are not ready to change your life. That's ok. Put the book down and revisit it when you are ready.

2. You are scared. Then jump straight to Part II, Day 1 and The Fear Process. Trust me, it will help.
3. You haven't got a life (well, let's face it, if you haven't got 30 minutes for yourself in a day, you haven't got one, really). Isn't it time you get one?

Excuses over? Good.

How to go through the 90 days

Part II of this book "90 days to your new career" is laid out as a journey for 90 consecutive days, establishing some daily habits which hopefully you'll keep on-going.

Don't be tempted to skip through it and do more than one day at the time. Instead of going fast, go deep into your feelings/fears and be honest with yourself.

Each day begins with a Monkey Mind/"dump the c*** off your brain into a page" exercise.

Say what?????? You read it right: The Monkey Mind Exercise.

Put it simply, this is outpouring streams of consciousness on a page (or more) to start the day with a clear mind. It is a means to an end with neither right nor wrong way of doing it.

I first heard of this exercise via Tim Ferriss in "Tools of Titans". He was inspired by Julia Cameron in her "The Artist Way: Morning Pages Journal".

Write a minimum of a page (you'll see, some days you won't be able to stop at that). I will just supply you with an opening sentence/word; a prompt and then you'll write anything and everything that comes to mind.

If you don't feel like doing it, force yourself: it is like therapy but free.

Each day ends with 3 things you are grateful for/appreciate related to the topic discussed for that day — it doesn't matter how small and apparently insignificant.

Instead of talking about the usual suspects though (*grateful for health, children, the dog , etc., etc.*) use this as an opportunity to review things in the context of the day's subject.

If you can't find anything to be grateful for/appreciate for that given subject, think again — you are not looking hard enough.

By looking for things to appreciate, you are firstly training your mind to look for positive aspects. Secondly, and most importantly, you begin to recognize how many more opportunities you/we, as women, have now compared to the past, many of which we take for granted.

When to start

You should really start on a Sunday (Day 1) with the "Fear" exercise to unroot your fears from the unconscious mind and bring them to the surface.

Owning and acknowledging fears is a very powerful first step to disempowering them. It is the fears that we ignore and that have power over us.

And then from Day 2 onwards, Mondays to Fridays, is reading and exercises — daily (we are talking about 20 minutes or 30 if you'll have a cup of tea whilst doing them).

This avoids the IDIOS fallacy. That is an acronym for *I'll do it on Saturday*, and it is a fallacy because a) you won't, and b) if you do, you'll hate it for eating up time in your weekend.

On weekends you are kind of free; I'm saying kind of because you should still do the Monkey Mind brain dump in the morning and the 3 things to be grateful for in the evening.

If you wish to re-read and go over the week, by all means do, but don't force yourself. Spend time resting, recharging your batteries, doing the things you love with the people you love (or your errands if you have to…).

Time to start.

"Go forth, my book, and help destroy the world as we know it"

RUSSELL BANKS

PART I

"Change starts from within.
There is no one to change
but Self.
Your only true limit is **YOU**.
STOP IT! It is all in your head!"

Laura Mariani

STOP IT! IT IS ALL IN YOUR HEAD

....

#SMASHYOURCEILING
TO SMASH THAT CEILING

BY LAURA MARIANI

LETTER TO THE READER

Women on Boards, or lack of them, is still a current topic — if you are looking at top global companies worldwide women in leadership represent 12% of the total (depending on what research is taken into consideration and the number of companies surveyed).

The International Women's Day's pledge for 2022 is #BreakTheBias (Imagine a gender equal world. A world free of bias, stereotypes, and discrimination - diverse, equitable, and inclusive - where difference is valued and celebrated).

Each year we go around the same merry-go-round, new legislation, new pledges, new campaigns and there we go again.

You know what? I'm sick and tired of pledges. Is this ever going to stop?

According to research carried out at the BI Norwegian Business School by Professor Øyvind L. Martinsen and Professor Lars Glasø, women are better suited at leadership than men based on five personality traits, which can be measured for effective leadership. The study surveyed more than 2,900 managers to ascertain leadership personality traits.

Women scored higher in:

- Initiative and clear communication
- Openness and ability to innovate
- Sociability and supportiveness and
- Methodical management and goal setting.

So, if women possess most of the qualities necessary to be a leader, what is stopping them? Lack of visible female leadership and role models has certainly played a part, same as cultural and family paradigms, sexism, racism, ageism and all other isms out there.

Human beings throughout history, however (including women) have overcome obstacles that seemed insurmountable to achieve their dreams/justice or whatever it is they wanted during times when over-coming these obstacles represented everything that was not "the right thing to do," during times when laws were against them.

Did this stop them? Of course not, they fought and found a way, because the what and why were bigger than the "No you can't".

There were people who accepted the way things were and conformed, still are, people that think that things are unfair, the state should do more, religion should do more, someone else should do more, always someone else.

You know what? It is time to STOP IT!!!
    Stop giving power to external forces and let them control your life.

STOP IT!

Smash that ceiling, and I mean the ceiling in your head, the only thing that is truly stopping you to achieve what you really want, and if that is being CEO of some company or Prime Minister/President or whatever, so be it.

Reading this book and seeing what it is all about and maybe getting some ideas might be your goal. But *my* goal is for you to realize that, once you have truly come to terms with what you really want for your life and why you really want it, once you have controlled your mind and believe, you will be unstoppable.

It is time to take charge and reboot your career and create the work-life that you truly want.

Laura xxx

BLAH BLAH BLAH ...

WHERE ARE WE NOW?

Global Overview

We cannot deny that boardroom diversity is increasing although women remain underrepresented. Looking at recent research from Credit Suisse more than 3,000 global companies found that women held 14.7% of board seats in 2015, up by 54% from 2010 (The CS Gender 3000: The Reward for Change - 2016).

In the Morgan Stanley Capital International (MSCI) study, Women on Boards: Global Trends in Gender Diversity on Corporate Boards, November 2015, out of the 4,218 companies covered women held 15% of board seats up from 12.4% the previous year (73.5% had at least one woman director and 20.1% had boards with at least three women) while in the Deloitte's analysis of nearly 6,000 companies in 49 countries (Women in the Boardroom: A Global Perspective) women held 12% of board seats, of which only 4% at board chair position.

When it comes to women on boards, the Consumer sector has higher representation than other sectors, (seems logical considering there is more direct exposure/contact with the actual consumers and women consumers drive a lot of purchases).

Credit Suisse found that the Consumer sector 16.3% of women on boards, while Finance ranked second, at 14.8% and Manufacturing had the least, at 11.6%.

Research from many worldwide organizations have found that three women or more are needed to create a "critical mass," which can lead to better financial performance yet only 20.1% have at least three women.

MSCI found that having three or more women changes the boardroom dynamics and "enhances the likelihood that women's voices and ideas are heard", also resulting in better financial results than those companies who had fewer like 16% higher Return on Sales (ROS), 26% higher Return on Invested Capital (ROIC) and higher Return on Equity (ROE) than companies without (10.1% vs. 7.4%), as well as a superior price-to-book ratio (1.76 vs. 1.56).

They also found incidentally that companies with fewer women on boards had more governance-related controversies than average.

Who does it better?

The highest percentages of women on boards can be found in the old continent with Norway (46.7%), France (34.0%), and Sweden (33.6%) leading the way and the lowest in Taiwan (4.5%), South Korea (4.1%), and Japan (3.5%) — source Credit Suisse.

Countries with specific targets, quotas, and penalties for not meeting regulations have nearly doubled the average percentage of women on boards including the aforementioned Norway, Iceland, Finland, and Sweden (+ 34%) compared to countries without those measures (+18%).

What about the Law?

In February 2017 UN Women, a division of the United Nations dedicated to gender equality and the empowerment of women, unveiled The

"Roadmap for Substantive Equality: 2030," in line with and supportive of the concerted global efforts to achieve the 2030 Agenda for Sustainable Development.

The purpose of the Roadmap is to repeal and/or amend discriminatory laws against women whilst ensuring that laws are supportive in general of gender equality & women's human rights.

The UN Women Roadmap for Substantive Equality: 2030 focuses not only in achieving legislative reform but equally, and more crucially, that they are put into practice.

The move from theory to practice, from the legislative framework to roll out and enforcement will require however global coordination among different types of international and regional organizations, governments and so on.

The current estimate is that around 90% of the countries worldwide have at least one or more discriminatory law in their legislative framework with many different examples not exclusive to gender pay gap or women in leadership but also failures to adequately tackle violence against women, sexual harassment in public spaces and participation in politics. Gender-discriminatory laws are often rooted in discriminatory social norms, which remain pervasive and are difficult to change.

When it comes to Europe, equality between women and men has rooted in the Rome Treaty as one of the European Union's fundamental values over sixty years ago. Despite this, the gender pay gap still exists with women earning 16.3% less than men across Europe and continuing to face a glass ceiling in reaching management and leadership positions (the European Commission is on track though to meet its own target of 40% female representation in senior and middle management positions by 2019).

. . .

Europe, in one way, is a pioneer of gender equality, having entrenched these fundamental rights into legislation. In the 2017 Gender Equality report (European Commission) it shows that the glass ceiling still exists with only France, Italy, Finland and Sweden having at least 30% women on the boards of large companies.

In the United Kingdom, there has been a cultural movement in British businesses with the number of women on FTSE 350 boards more than doubling since 2011 and no more all-male boards in the FTSE 100.

In 2010 a government-back commission (the Davies Review led by Lord Davies of Abersoch) was introduced to assess the underrepresentation of women on boards.

In 2011 the "Women on Boards" report was released pushing the issue of gender equality forward with a voluntary target of 25% women on the boards of FTSE 100 companies by the end of 2015 which was met. This progress, however, was made under a voluntary & business-led frame-work, without Government or EU legislative intervention.

In 2015 Lord Davies released his five-year summary and raised the target again this time to 33% by 2020 on FTSE 350 boards.

The percentage of women in FTSE 100 boardrooms currently stands at 26.1%, but the UK is still seventh across the main international stock markets, behind Norway and France.

2016 saw the percentage of women on FTSE 100 boards increase to 26%, which is significantly more than in March 2015 when the Female FTSE report recorded 23.5%, but similar to October 2015 when the Davies closing report recorded 26.1%. The percentage of women holding FTSE

100 non-executive directorships is 31.4%, compared to 28.5% in March 2015 and 31.4% in October 2015.

The percentage of women in executive directorships on FTSE 100 boards is 9.7%, compared to 8.6% in March 2015 and 9.6% in October 2015. These trends point to steady progress compared to March 2015 but to a relative stagnation of the pace of change since October 2015 (Cranfield School of Management – The Female FTSE Board Report 2016).

Professor Susan Vinnicombe, CBE, said: "The focus on boards must be preserved as the pace of change has not kept up after the Davies closing report. In order to hit the 33% board target by 2020, chairmen and search consultants must ensure the board appointment process remains robust, transparent and gender-inclusive."

ONCE UPON A TIME

A woman's place

W hat a "woman's place" is or seen to be has varied throughout history from warriors, powerful priestesses, and political leaders to portrayals inferior to men and I think looking briefly, very briefly (I'm not going to bore you with history and a historical portrait — it is not the purpose of this book) at the position of women at different points in history, it can show us how our society has grown and changed and help us to understand the present, including barriers.

Women have gained and lost power at different times in history; if we look at back at the early times in Christian church, women could hold positions of influence equal to men, (even though the Da Vinci Code is a work of fiction, there are indications that Mary Magdalene was once a significant religious leader — an apocryphal gospel of Mary Magdalene was discovered in the late nineteenth century in Egypt – having a gospel in itself is of significance here).

· · ·

The fourth and fifth centuries AD, however, saw the degrading of women in the writings of people such as Tertullian, Saint Augustine and Saint Jerome blaming Eve, and consequently by association all women, for the downfall of humanity.

The late 1500s is generally seen as the beginning of Modern History with the Renaissance. Yes, women were painted and portrayed beautifully, but this did not really affect women on a day to day basis.

A woman's place was defined as the homemaker with strict expectations: women could not vote and were discouraged in owning a business.

Women of aristocratic families (with properties) were often forced/offered into political marriages where all their property then transferred to their husband.

The biggest gains in equality had to wait until the twentieth century, for example, with the Suffragettes successful campaign for women being granted the right to vote. World War one and two also showed that women could contribute to the economy and could work both inside and outside the home, taking men's places in factories.

The sixties and seventies and the advent of feminism further changed some of society's perceptions and, most importantly changed women's own beliefs (*I did say I was going to be brief, moving on*).

WHAT ARE THE BARRIERS?

Cultural, religious & family paradigms

It is difficult to talk about religion without insulting /annoying someone somewhere and without being disputed on the interpretation/miss-interpretation of the scripture/s and this section is not meant in any way to be a pontification of the good/evil in religion/s and or the ultimate guide to mainstream religions' views on women.

This section is to recognize and acknowledge that religion has played/is playing and will continue to play a big part in the way different groups of people perceive themselves and others and their definition of "what good looks like" including women and their role in society and that there is a correlation between the two.

Many religions share the same characterizations and expectations of a traditional female role:

- Raise and teach children
- Maintain a Godly household

- Assist the husband decisions
- Retain and care for family & familial assets.

In Judaism interestingly God is considered both male and female and, where female responsibilities are concerned, there is less emphasis on gender roles. However, women are expected to perform more intellectual tasks, while men take care of physical tasks (thirteen women have served as cabinet ministers since the state of Israel was established).

I'm not saying that religion is the problem but mainly one of the potential restrictions. Sexism, misogyny and patriarchy and attitudes exist often entangled with other social and political factors and ways of thinking, including religion.

When I say patriarchy I mean a system of power relations between men and women, where men and women are complicit and agential, and which privileges particular kinds of gender and sexual identities (usually heterosexual men) over others.

These power relations are part of the inner structural personal system with your entire personal image built on this — your belief foundation — which determines what you believe you can and cannot do, how should you do it and why.

For women who wish to have children, there are also the obviously added barriers of going through the gestation period, the birth and consequent time needed to care for a newborn and beyond.

There is the physical barrier (not everyone has an easy pregnancy and is able to continue to perform to the same level/with the same intensity —

the time-off pre/post — part) together with the childcare requirements.

Society is made of tribal congregations (religious and secular institutions, communities and families) all with their individual, sometimes divergent and sometimes mutually supportive views of a "woman's place," a "mother's duty" and "the right way of doing things".

The "good girl syndrome"

Although there is definitely the outer game of society/family paradigms and so on, there is also a far more important inner game, your own perceptions, your own decisions, belief systems that drive behavior and choices made — the "good girl syndrome".

Rachida Dati comes to mind, the French Justice Minister under French President Nicolas Sarkozy who went back to work five days after having her first child by Caesarean section.

Seeing her going back as what is perceived (by whom?) too soon started a barrage and ping-pong of comments and articles, some quite bitching and derogative and some alleging bullying from Sarkozy (and the worse ones were from women).

Even the way she was described ("impossibly glamorous and thin") had negative connotations (like what — all new mothers must look/are fat and frumpy??).

Better still, people were discussing if she is *"right to put the demands of her career ahead of her child? Or is she crazy to miss out on some of the most precious months of her life? "* like there is only ONE way of being a mother AND a career woman at the same time.

TELL ME WHAT YOU WANT, WHAT YOU REALLY REALLY WANT

SUCCESS IS A RELATIVE THING

Success means so many things to so many people; if you don't define what good (or great) looks like, you will be always chasing something, the next shiny object, unachievable targets and never quite satisfied.

WHAT DOES SUCCESS MEAN TO YOU?

Take some time to think about what does it really mean to you:

- a job well done?
- position/power?
- how would you know you have arrived?

OR

is it rather the feeling that THE job will give you:
- recognition?
- respect from colleagues / family / friends?
- financial security/money? fulfilling expectations (family/friends/ society)?

What is the destination and why? What will it give you?

WHAT IS YOUR WHY?

The Maslow Hierarchy of Needs

Maslow Hierarchy of Needs is one of the best-known motivational theories trying to understand what drives "humans".

Abraham Maslow, a human psychologist, explained this concept in his 1943 paper "A Theory of Human Motivation" and his subsequent book "Motivation and Personality" stating that our actions are motivated so to satisfy certain needs.

Maslow suggests that people are motivated to fulfill basic needs before moving on to the more advanced needs, trying to understand what makes people happy and the things that they do/would to fulfill their needs.

His belief was that people have an innate need and desire to be all they can be but to do so they must meet first a number of more basic needs (the most common representation of this theory is often a pyramid, moving from most basic needs at the bottom to the most complex at the top).

According to Maslow there are five different levels starting at the lowest known as physiological needs.

The bottom of the pyramid has the most basic physical requirements including the need for food, water, sleep, and warmth, and once these are satisfied and people progress up the pyramid, and then these become more and more psychological and social, and so on, all the way to self-actualization, e.g., growing and developing as a person in order to achieve own potential.

Physiological, security, social, and esteem needs are what we would call deficiency needs, arising from lack and satisfying them is important in order to avoid unpleasant situations.

On the other hand at the highest levels of the pyramid are growth needs which do not stem from deprivation, but rather from a desire to grow as a person.

The need for security and safety then becomes primary and it is all about control and order in our lives and consequent behaviors (financial security, health and wellness, safety against accidents and injury).

The need for appreciation and respect, e.g., gaining the respect and appreciation of others leads to the need to accomplish things and then have efforts recognized together with the feeling of accomplishment and prestige, self-esteem and personal worth.

Self-actualization - "What a man can be, he must be," is the need people have to achieve their full potential as human beings.

. . .

"It may be loosely described as the full use and exploitation of talents, capabilities, potentialities, etc. Such people seem to be fulfilling themselves and to be doing the best that they are capable of doing... They are people who have developed or are developing to the full stature of which they are capable" (Abraham Maslow).

Similarly to Maslow Tony Robbins, in his programs and many books, talks about in a more fluid & less hierarchical way the same drivers of human behaviors:

- Certainty and security
- Uncertainty and variety
- Significance
- Love & Connection
- Growth
- Contribution.

It is important here not to be too rigid about the standard progression of the needs within the pyramid: what is more important or indeed essential to one person might not be to others (except perhaps the basic physiological needs that are vital to our survival and essential to the survival and propagation of the species).

My point here is that, on top of the infrastructural belief system based on cultural, religious (or non-religious) & family paradigms, there are basic human needs that need to be fulfilled.

WHAT IS THE PRICE?

Everyone pays a price

There is a perception that women (even more so women with children) pay a price to rise to the top of an organization/field , etc., (as opposed to it is easy for men?).

Let's face it:
Leadership requires 100% commitment-
Everyone pays a price. You know what?

STOP IT!

Stop making excuses, It is all B*****t.

In the 2015 Global Entrepreneurship Monitor (GEM) Special Report on Women Entrepreneurship, women's entrepreneurship rose by 6% world-wide in the last two years. According to the 2016 Kauffman Index of

Startup Activity, in the United States women make up 40% of new entre-preneurs (highest since 1996).

In the MasterCard Index of Women Entrepreneurs 2017 (MIWE) women's business ownership across the 54 markets measured make up between 25-35% of total business owners .

In Chapter 1 – *Where are we now – Global Overview* we have seen the statistics on women on boardroom representation according to some recent reports (respectively 14,7% Credit Suisse, 15% Morgan Stanley and 12% Deloitte using different samples).

The barriers are the same including childcare.

PERFECTION IS BORING - BE AWESOME INSTEAD

Wonder Woman does not exist

The idea that you should take as little maternity leave as possible, work until your waters break beneath your desk, never complain of sickness, swollen ankles and/or backache, and then go back to work fast and/or go back to work and (as much as you love your baby and being a mum) enjoying being back to work and more than baby-talk, but feeling guilty all the way through it, and then coming back home and be the "perfect" wife/partner/significant other (whatever you like to be called) and cooking, cleaning, tidying and putting the baby to bed is ludicrous.

Silence your inner critic — do you and what works for you.

However, the practicality of looking after a child and who is going to do it post return to work exists and unfortunately, no matter the progress made recently, we can't deny that women, in the vast majority of cases, still bear the burden of household and family responsibility. That means women in general and even more so women aspiring to leadership positions have to juggle even more than their male counterparts.

Now all the employment laws on maternity, paternity, shared parental leave and flexible working mean absolutely nothing unless men take up/opt for these opportunities and support their partner/wife/significant other. It is easy to criticize "society," the government, businesses , etc., and ask for more laws, more rules to aid women coming back to work and pursuing a career/leadership and talk about what "men should do more".

Society is made of families and individuals and the change will happen and can happen — starting from your family and your partner taking up a fair share of childcare/household duties and so on.

Relationships do break up sometime but this does not nullify paternal responsibilities and accountabilities in raising children irrespectively of how much you might dislike/hate/can't stand your ex-partner and their new life (of course there might be fathers/parents who are unfit although let's consider this for argument sake to be an exception than the rule).

Think of your family unit as a business with two main shareholders whereby the decisions made are for the best interest of the "business"/family unit whilst not stifling ambitions and/or disadvantage either and/or both shareholders .

Too many times men request flexible working and or parental leave (and/or maternity leave) only and exclusively when their wife/partner/significant other already earns more than they do, far more rarely when they are on equal earning footing or thereabouts .The discussion needs to happen about your mutual ambition and career aspiration together with shared responsibilities and potential support needed (in what forms and by whom).

True feminism means accepting both the reality of motherhood, and celebrating its real value personally and to society as a whole but also having equal opportunities and being able to make a choice on how you would like to deal with your career and motherhood without having to apologize if you are ambitious and want to go back to work as soon as, or take a few years off.

THINK OUTSIDE THE BOX:
WHAT BOX?

THINK THE PART

The Journey

OK, you want to be CEO of a (Global) Company or Director of Paperclips (whatever takes your fancy); you can map out how you can get there and the first point is a "thinking map-journey".

What do I mean by that?

Each role from junior management to leadership/director/board level has different thinking requirements: from the here and now action-oriented operational/problem solving way of thinking to the tactical/fluid and then strategic/long term/future forward way of thinking, anticipating what customers might want/need in 10/20 years time whilst staying original and true to brand AND beating the competition.

Plus cross-functional and P&L/financial implications thinking (I'm going to address knowledge/skills and behaviors in later chapters).

. . .

This is when mapping comes useful e.g. gathering job descriptions from junior management to the highest functional /board director/VP and CEO to be able to see and understand the difference in requirements (I suggest here to start with your own function, whatever that is - HR, Finance, Marketing for example — to make it easier-although getting some other examples at the top it is useful to understand the cross-functional thinking/activities etc.).

This is for several reasons:

Understanding the depth and breadth of thinking required at CEO level helps you to connect and understand the company overall direction (there is a very interesting story about John F. Kennedy visiting NASA headquarters for the first time in 1961 and his meeting with a cleaner who was then mopping the floor. When JFK introduced himself and asked him what he did at NASA, he replied: "I'm helping put a man on the moon!!") – remember those Maslow's needs? The desire to be part of something bigger and gain purpose?

Understanding the level/type of thinking required helps you to understand the potential decision/s that will have to be taken (without being patronizing, it can be lonely at the top when you have to make incredibly unpopular decisions that affects thousand of people sometimes negatively but they are for the long term longevity of the organization and its greater good) — and the compromises that one has to make.

If making these types of decisions makes you uncomfortable it is time perhaps to rethink if you really want it. Yes, you could be the conscience in the boardroom — nevertheless, sometime, these decisions must be made and you need to be prepared to do so.

You can identify the top areas (of thinking) that also appear in your own job description, and in each one, and start with the ones more aligned to your strengths (I follow the Tim Ferriss way of thinking — it is better to focus on your strengths than your weakness — this is because in working on your strengths it will be easier and quicker to maximize the improvements and achieve greatness while working on weaknesses would take much longer and you'd become at maximum average).

Read and understand — what are the verbs used?

What is the difference between current role to ultimate role/next role, etc.? How can you apply a higher level of thinking and expand your mind in your current role?

Depending where you are right now in your career you can see how many steps along the way whilst keeping an eye on the end game.

And keeping in mind the end destination helps when making career decisions along the way, as each role — upward or sideways — should be a stepping-stone to the ultimate goal.

Tip:

You can start applying a higher level thinking to the You (family/life , etc.) Company: start looking at your own life/family , etc., as a Plc. (remember the two shareholders and parental/household responsibilities?):

- What is your brand/what is important to you?
- Who are your main stakeholders/customers/consumers?
- How can you satisfy their need whilst staying true to you?
- What's the long term plan?

Identify your assets, liabilities, risks, income streams & financial goals (start a Profit & Loss sheet?)and so on.

Your life is like your own business ...

Bridge the Gap

"You are the average of the five people
you surround yourself with" – **Napoleon Hill.**

This is true financially, emotionally, standard wise and is applicable here too. Finding and connecting with people who are already there, asking questions on their decision-making process — what, why, how they make decisions, critical paths.

"[Emerging] leaders need mentors to guide them, but they also need a network of
peers, to reassure them that they are not on the path alone".
Alyse Nelson – President and CEO, Vital Voices.

I definitely agree that leaders need mentors; I don't know if I necessarily agree with a network of peers being a practical tool to help your way to the top. Indeed your peers share your issues and your struggle, which means they haven't got a solution as yet.

There are professional bodies out there for almost any occupation and what they do is not just provide a "stamp of approval" and add to individual credibility but also provide a community to link up to, exchange views/ask questions, receive support and easily available credible resources and industry trends.

Nevertheless not everyone rises to the top even belonging to these bodies, and this is even more applicable for women.

Mirror Mirror

If you want to be the best, you need to learn from the best – I have not invented this phrase — you can hear it from the lips of the most successful entrepreneurs, CEOs, billionaires out there. And that is the point.

You need someone who has been there, seen it, done it and got the t-shirt so to speak and you can emulate exactly what he or she has done and shortcut your way to success. This is applicable to both people you associate with on a daily basis and to choosing mentors to speed your journey.

> *"If you want to be successful,*
> *Find someone who has achieved the results you want*
> *And copy what they do*
> *And you'll achieve the same results",*
> **Tony Robbins**.

Women may share a lot of things (the blogosphere explosion is a testament to this) but having a strong mentor usually is not one, men seem to be more apt at networking with purpose and connecting with people who can help them rather than just sharing experiences.

Having a mentor is one the most critical factors for continuous growth and accelerated success. Picking both men and women mentors that tell you not what you want to hear but what you need to hear is priceless: men will give you an insight in the way things are (if we are to believe the *"old boys club"* exists) and they can be an inside ally and advocate. Women can guide you on potential obstacles they faced specifically as female and how they dealt with them.

. . .

Mirror, Mirror, here and in subsequent chapters, also refers to the NeuroLinguistic Programming technique of Mirroring and Matching to build Rapport .

Mirroring is one of the most useful NLP techniques there are, is innate and even chimps use mirroring within their groups. Conscious and deliberate use of it can help to break down barriers, in negotiations, meetings, new environments, interviews , etc.

It is also useful to determine whether people are visual, audial, or kinaesthetic (you do so by listening to their language patterns) and consequently adapt your presentation and communication/language style to suit the specific audience and have more impact.

State	Primary sense	Language patterns
Visual	Sight	I see; it looks good
Audial	Hearing	Sounds good; that rings a bell
Kinaesthetic	Feeling	That doesn't feel right; I can't put my finger on it

LOOK THE PART

The Power of First Impressions

Accounting to Malcolm Gladwell, in "Blink: The Power of Thinking Without Thinking" people make up their minds about people they meet for the first time instantaneously or in two-seconds — can you imagine?!

Research also suggests that first impressions can be so powerful that they can become more important and believable than fact.

Recent studies presented at the Society of Personality and Social Psychology annual conference in Texas found that even when told whether a person was gay or straight, people identified a person's sexual orientation based on how they looked — irrespectively of the facts blatantly contradicting their impression.

"We judge books by their covers, and we can't help but do it," said Nicholas Rule, Ph.D., of the University of Toronto. "With effort, we can overcome this to some extent, but we are continually tasked with needing to correct ourselves."

Furthermore, the less time we have to make our judgments, the more likely we are to go with our gut, even over fact.

As soon as one sees another person, an impression is formed. This happens so quickly that what we see can sometimes dominate what we know," Rule said.

Additionally, the first impression formed online is often more negative than a first impression formed in person.

First impressions do matter for both good and bad depending if the first meeting was fine or not — positive = social cohesion; negative = potential biases and social prejudice — like an halo effect.

Our appearance makes an instant statement to others about who we are and what we are about.

I know that, when this subject is approached, women especially get all uppity saying appearance doesn't matter, shouldn't matter, blah blah blah …

It does and it does with people in the same way that it does with products.

Manufacturing is one very good example with factories many times producing consumer goods with exact same recipe/specification but with different labels at the end of the production line and the products are then perceived/received in a completely different manner by consumers (including sometime a substantial price point difference) and this is both because of the perception of quality (based on the branding/marketing of the different labels/brands) but also what buying certain brands says about us and how we want to be seen.

Think about that.

Leading Lady

Are you aware of what are you projecting right now? Is this aligned to the "new role" that you are aiming for (according to your map)?

Having knowledge about yourself and how you come across will enable you to create a personal style that goes beyond clothes and encompasses your approach to your career and life and how you feel about yourself.

Once you have decided the type of position/s you want to go for, the clout it is meant to have, the potential stakeholders/clients for that role (taking for example a CFO position — it need to be credible in front of Government officials, investors and shareholders and shout reliability) and the industry and its related branding, and also what kind of person and woman you are and want to be and the kind of life you want, then you'll need to carefully analyze and choose what features to emphasize and which ones not.

Having a capsule wardrobe where everything works with each other and that makes you look your best whilst projecting the image appropriate for your new position at all times means that you are ready for all occasions and feel confident at all times and believing it convinces everyone else too.

Perfect your image and showcase it everyday .

Consistency is the key — having one look at work and one in your private life could be problematic especially if they are very different.

Do remember social media .

Mirror Mirror

At this point we need to consider both "creating" your new image that is congruent and supportive of your ambition whilst changing your current workplace perception of you and "helping" them to start seeing you in a new light.

· · ·

We have looked at the steps necessary for the "creating" above and now it is a matter of slowly transitioning into your new image and then perhaps a big reveal after a period of absence (holiday?).

The two might seem a contradiction in terms — slow transition and big reveal — but they are not. I'm talking here about the subtle transformation using the mirror and matching discussed in the Think The Part chapter and slowly shifting perceptions.

You have already chosen the people who are in the type of position/s that you would like to be in as "thinking" role models and mentors who can be your advocates during the change. Start also observing their style — how they dress for interviews/meetings/everyday ; is their style conservative? Creative? Aligned with the company brand?

Mirror and match — thinking — mirror and match — dress — mirror and match.

Creating a new persona congruent with your aspirations is not only useful to improve people's opinion of you but also to actually improve your performance.

Stay with me ...

In a 2012 study at Northwestern University's Kellogg School of Management researcher found that wearing certain clothes that were associated with certain qualities enhanced the person's performance.

The specific example in the study evolved around individuals instructed to wear white coats described either as "lab coats" or as "artistic painters' coats" (actually identical to the lab coats) while they performed a task; a third group however was shown a lab coat before being asked to perform the task so to demonstrated that wearing the coats was what would make the difference .

The three groups were asked to perform a test that was designed to test their sustained attention.

The researchers found that people wearing the "lab coat" found significantly more differences in the same amount of time than the "artists," meaning that their attention was increased while wearing the coat concluding that dressing for success is contingent to both the representational meaning and the physical experience of wearing the clothes".

How about that?

ACT THE PART

Fake it Til You Make it

Confidence has a huge effect on performance — pretending you are confident until you gain the experience or tools necessary and is real might feel artificial and forced in the beginning, but soon will become more natural — remember the mind can be tricked — acting a certain way allows your brain to "rehearse" new ways until you have actually learned what you need to and turned into the real deal

Mirror Mirror

Mimicking (I know, mirror and matching again) people who display the required skill sets and behaviors, even if you worry about appearing like a fraud is very helpful, according to research.

Professor of organizational behavior Herminia Ibarra wrote in the *Harvard Business Review* about such (her) research "By viewing ourselves as works in progress, we multiply our capacity to learn, avoid being pigeonholed, and ultimately become better leaders. We're never too experienced to fake it till we learn it".

THE HERO JOURNEY

THE POWER OF ROLE MODELS

In every story, every hero is helped through his/her journey when meeting a mentor and then allies along the way.

Well, this is my way to provide for you some virtual mentors/allies/role models to show you their "call to adventure", their crossing of thresholds together with perhaps tests, allies and maybe enemies.

I believe in women empowering women and in the power of the mind — you create your own reality — and this is my gift to you:

THE HERO JOURNEY of some real women.

Not famous but superstars nevertheless because they have done it and they are living their life on their terms. They are women at different stages of their journey so, when you are feeling down and out, discouraged in some way, you can get some inspiration and let it flow…

"Believe in yourself, You Can"

WOMEN IN BUSINESS: VISIBLE LEADERSHIP INTERVIEWS

NATASHA MAKHIJANI

Natasha Makhijani is the Founder and now CEO of the **Oliver Sanderson Group Plc.**, a Search & Selection agency across different disciplines and industries which she has now taken to Group/Plc. status.

She was nominated for the Diversity Champion of the Year Award, Women in Logistics two years in a row.

Natasha is also the CEO of **Snapp CV**, a mobile job board, also the brainchild of Natasha, where users can log on and swipe through vacancies on offer, then apply by simply clicking "apply now" button and record a 30 second profile video of themselves, which is then sent directly to the Hiring Company/Manager.

Websites:
www.oliversanderson.com
www.snappcvgroup.com

1. When you were a child what was your dream job and why?

My dream job was always to open my own business but not in recruitment but in the Asian Bridal Industry, as I am a very creative person.

My dream was to open a shop East meets West in Chelsea or Knightsbridge and cater for the one stop shop for the bridal industry from the dress, to make up to the Jewelry for the Asian, English, Arabic bride and so forth.

2. Can you tell me the time that you started to consider yourself successful?

From a young age I was always hard working, confident and ambitious. I believe if you work hard and have faith you will succeed. The road may not be easy, there will be ups and downs but continue and your path will change its course to success.

3. I'm sure like every business/business person you have faced adversity: how do you motivate yourself and force through the worst times?

My belief, my values, my family and my passion for life. The fact that if I have struggled and seen the worst times which believe me I have, I pick myself up, smile and continue as I know it is a passing phase and there is sunshine at the end of the tunnel.

4. What are the best things about your job?

. . .

My business is a people led industry, I have fun and do what I do best: change people's lives. Working with clients and candidates and making them happy, building a relationship with them there is nothing more rewarding than this.

5. As Tony Robbins says, *"Success leaves clues"*: what are your daily/weekly habits?

I am very focused and disciplined. I train three times a week at the gym and practice yoga, eat healthy, work long hours and always deliver to my clients and candidates. I would say to run your own business you need to be disciplined and focus. It means sacrifice in certain areas of your life. Success comes with hard work and confidence and to never give up. It will not be handed to anyone on a plate.

6. What do you think is the most significant barrier to female leadership?

The most significant barrier to female leadership is that the boardroom is still very male led although several businesses have now become very diverse. The barrier to entry is that women must balance being a business leader, a wife, and a mother and manage the house.

There are some amazing women out there that have achieved all of this and some that have had to sacrifice certain aspects of their life to reach the top. Industry has opened these doors for women but I still feel a lot more support can be given.

Look at how many women are lost to the world of work once they become mothers. Industry and the workplace need to make this easier for those women who would like to pursue both avenues.

. . .

The Female leader should not be lost and when she reaches the top feel guilty, as she cannot fulfill all her duties as a woman. She should be given support in all areas.

Society is changing but we still have a long way to go.

7. What women inspire you and why?

- Susie Robinson – VP of HR EMEA - DHL
- Tanith Dodge – Group HRD Value Retail and ex M & S. Group
- Sharon Doherty - Vodafone Global Organization & People Development Director.

These three women are an inspiration to me now and as a young woman from my earlier career.

I have watched and followed how they have managed to balance and achieve great things in their careers, professionally, personally and be successful in the boardroom.

A real inspiration to women across the globe. These three women are shining examples that there is nothing you cannot achieve.

8. What advice would you give to your 16year old self?

Believe in yourself, You can.

. . .

9. Your instant mindfulness fix…

Yoga, peace and to smile.

10. And finally, something frivolous: best thing about being a woman…

Handbags and Shoes.

But most of all being able to have my hair and nails done every week. You don't need makeup but if your hair looks good, nails are done and eyebrows are shaped you are ready to face the world and conquer all.

Top Takeaways from Natasha:

- Believe in yourself, You Can
- Work hard and have faith
- In difficult times pick yourself up, smile and continue (it will pass): there is sunshine at the end of the tunnel
- Love what you do and have fun with it
- Be focused and disciplined — success comes with hard work; nobody is going to hand it over to you on a plate.

RACHEL DIPPER

Rachel Dipper is the CEO and Founder at **We Are Fetching**, a free mobile app that brings the sharing economy to childcare with an integrated schools platform that gives complete visibility of who is approved to collect each child with photos and contact details.

The app provides live updates on who is collecting that day, reducing administration and ensuring fewer late pick ups. Rachel has extensive B2C marketing experience across retail and professional services.

Prior to founding **We Are Fetching**, Rachel was Chief Marketing Officer at Mettle and Vice President of Marketing & Partnership at OneDome.

Website:
  www.wearefetching.com

1. When you were a child what was your dream job and why?

. . .

This is going to sound really odd, but I always wanted to work in a big shiny office block. In my imagination, I would walk in and everyone would know me and say good morning.

I must have watched the film "Working Girl" with Melanie Griffiths at least 20 times when I was growing up, which probably had an impact. It is very 80s but I think that unfortunately, some of the challenges that Griffiths' character faces in the film can still be found in workplaces today.

2. Can you tell me the time that you started to consider yourself successful?

My previous role was for a global property partnership and, even though I only worked on residential, senior people from other areas of the business started greeting me around the building and commenting on my work. I really wanted to say, "How do you even know who I am?" but I thought it best just to roll with it.

3. I'm sure like every business/business person you have faced adversity: how do you motivate yourself and force through the worst times?

My husband and son are a great support. My husband in particular is very good at pointing out the side of an issue that I haven't seen. It aggravates me intensely at the time, but he helps me get some perspective. My son is only small, so he just offers a big hug!

Ultimately though, I've always had an "I'll show them!" attitude to work, and will not be beaten by professional challenges — or challengers. Some people call it being bloody minded.

. . .

4. What are the best things about your job?

Some nights I can't sleep because of the excitement about what I will do the next day. I have seen so many people looking sideways and copying their competition. We Are Fetching brings the sharing economy to child-care, saving parents time and stress . I work very collaboratively with the team and no idea is off the table at this stage.

5. As Tony Robbins says, *"Success leaves clues"*: what are your daily/weekly habits?

I always listen to something motivational on the way to the office. I have a 20-minute walk from the Bank so it is either a podcast that will inspire me in my work, or some cheesy pop that gets me pumped up for the day ahead. At the moment, one of my favorite podcasts is Masters Of Scale with Reid Hoffman.

6. What do you think is the most significant barrier to female leadership?

I believe a lot of it is down to recruitment. I don't think that there is an inherent sexism — most people say that they would like to hire more women if they are the best candidates. However, I think people are often subconsciously biased towards people that are like themselves, and so the problem perpetuates.

7. What women inspire you and why?

. . .

Of course everyone loves Sheryl Sandberg – she has done amazing things at Facebook, and to promote women in business. I also really respect Roisin Donnelly – the former Brand Director at Procter & Gamble.

I heard her speak at a WACL (Women in Advertising & Communications, London) event and thought she was amazing. She left P&G last year and is now a Non-Executive Director for a number of companies. If she were reading this, I would love to take her to lunch.

8. What advice would you give to your 16year old self?

Don't wait for anything to come to you — go out and get it. Whether it's a new circle of friends, a great body or a career; nothing worth doing is easy.

9. Your instant mindfulness fix...

Being near water. I live in the Docklands so I'm lucky enough to have the Thames on my doorstep. I have been known to go down onto the riverbed when the tide is out — it is extraordinarily peaceful. People think that London is busy and crowded, but there are some real havens if you know where to look.

10. And finally, something frivolous: best thing about being a woman...

Drinking wine with my girlfriends. There is a very strict "no judgment" rule amongst my friends who have children.

Understanding other people's challenges rather than leaping to judge them has changed my whole perspective on life.

. . .

Top Takeaways from Rachel:

- Don't be beaten by challenges - You Can!
- Don't wait for anything to come to you - Go and Get It!
- Listen to something motivational before your day starts - Get pumped for the day ahead — whatever works for you.Find a peaceful haven
- Understanding others challenges can change your whole perspective.

JACKIE SMITHEN

J ackie Smithen is a Senior Human Resources Director at GlaxoSmithKline (**GSK**), a science-led global healthcare company with three world-leading businesses that researches, develops and manufactures innovative pharmaceutical medicines, vaccines and consumer healthcare products.

Website:
   www.gsk.com

1. When you were a child what was your dream job and why?

As a small child I wanted to be a teacher but I think that was largely because it was the job I came into contact with most.

As a teenager I wanted to be a translator as I had found a love of language and thought it was really cool to be able to connect two parties who couldn't communicate.

. . .

2. Can you tell me the time that you started to consider yourself successful?

Probably about eight years into my career. I had started on a graduate training program and for the early part of my career I didn't recognize the potential that others saw in me. It was only when I found myself in a role where I was leading a team and influencing others in the Business that I started to recognize the impact I was having which made me feel successful.

3. I'm sure like every business/business person you have faced adversity: how do you motivate yourself and force through the worst times?

You've got to enjoy what you are doing day-to-day otherwise no amount of motivation really helps! I look for small successes and little triumphs on a daily basis — not every day is full of monumental achievements and sometimes it's the small things and short conversations which help you to nudge things in the right direction.

4. What are the best things about your job?

Flexibility – that works both ways for me and the Company.

Variety – I love spinning plates even if it means that sometimes I end up picking up the pieces!

Autonomy – the freedom to choose what I work on next and how I approach things is energizing.

5. As Tony Robbins says, "Success leaves clues": what are your daily/weekly habits?

. . .

I try to work one day a week away from the office and use that time to work on different tasks (usually things which need me to really concentrate).

I am an extrovert so love the interactions that being in the office offers, but recognize that sometimes I need to step away from the hubbub and just allow myself time to think!

6. What do you think is the most significant barrier to female leadership?

Self-doubt. Personally I often think about whether I am the right person for a task or whether someone else might be better suited and it has taken me a while to accept good coaching advice that "I am more than enough as I am".

7. What women inspire you and why?

It may be clichéd but my mum was definitely a big inspiration for me. She worked hard all her life but managed to put her family first. She also had a great ability to connect with people from all walks of life, and was comfortable in her own skin.

8. What advice would you give to your 16year old self?

Worry less about what you will be and where you will end up. I didn't appreciate at 16 what it meant to be opportunistic and thought everything needed to be planned and mapped out. My working life has shown me the opposite is true!

. . .

9. Your instant mindfulness fix...

If you find yourself writing reams of notes when you are with someone — stop! Chances are you are not really present in the conversation.

10. And finally something frivolous: best thing about being a woman...

The shopping gene — luckily for me my daughter has also inherited it.

Top Takeaways from Jackie:

- You are more than enough as you are
- Enjoy what you are doing day by day
- Look for small successes and little triumphs daily — celebrate
- Allow yourself time to think
- Be present in the moment.

EMMAJANE TAYLOR-MORAN

Emmajane Taylor-Moran is a Director and Employment Lawyer at **Rebel Law Ltd.**, providing tailored employment law and HR advice and services to companies and individuals.

Emmajane specializes in dispute resolution, settlement agreements, furlough, redundancies, employment tribunals and providing supporting guidance to clients through difficult times.

Prior to **Rebel Law**, Emmajane was Partner and Head of Employment Law at Gelbergs LLP.

Emmajane volunteers at various legal surgeries, is a regular speaker and provides training workshops and seminars to employers o various legal topics in a digestible, interesting and interactive way. She is also the Chair of the Islington Chamber of Commerce (at time of publication).

Website:
    www.rebel-law.co.uk

· · ·

1. When you were a child what was your dream job and why?

When I was a little girl, my first career inclinations were towards literature and teaching, as I loved books with a passion.

I learned to read before I went to school and would read everything I could get hold of. I remember my mum telling me that I would make a good lawyer because I could argue for England! Now, as I am indeed a lawyer (thanks mum!) I can combine my interest in documents and my persuasive arguing skills!

2. Can you tell me the time that you started to consider yourself successful?

For me, it was a real pinnacle of my career to be invited to be a Partner at Gelbergs. I felt that the Partners trusted in me and my abilities to not only be a good lawyer but also a good leader and a good business person. In terms of "considering myself successful" that is an on-going objective — in my industry you are only as good as your last case/client/billing month, so I am constantly on my toes, challenging myself to do better.

3. I'm sure like every business/business person you have faced adversity: how do you motivate yourself and force through the worst times?

The best job is the one that you love so much that you get up every day and it doesn't feel like "work," and where your colleagues are your support network and you all pull together to keep each other motivated, sane and happy. I am incredibly lucky in both of these respects, and that is really motivating.

. . .

4. What are the best things about your job?

Without a doubt the best thing about my job is the people I work with —
both my clients and my colleagues. I also have a competitive streak and
love winning, so when I get a good outcome for a client, whether it is
negotiating a good deal to settle their case, or succeeding in tribunal,
then that gives me great satisfaction in a job well done.

**5. As Tony Robbins says, *"Success leaves clues"*: what are your
daily/weekly habits?**

I try and look after myself — my biggest weakness is getting so lost in
work that I don't take a break or hydrate properly throughout the day. So
I recognize this and try to rectify it. I also have a lot going on in my head
at one time, juggling lots of cases and clients, so to avoid getting overwhelmed and forgetting things, I make daily to-do lists. It frees up the
RAM in my head from too much mental clutter, so I can focus on doing
one thing at a time, and doing it well.

**6. What do you think is the most significant barrier to female
leadership?**

The feminist in my head wants to say that it is the patriarchal society that
we have inherited, where we still have such a long way to go to achieve
real equality. But I think as well as that, *it is us ourselves.*

As women, we often don't do enough to put ourselves forward, and
to build the confidence we should have in our skills.

We too often accept that we must sacrifice our careers for our families
because our partners are not expected to.

. . .

This is why I mentor young professional mothers through the CityParents scheme, because I am passionate about breaking down barriers, both in society and within ourselves.

7. What women inspire you and why?

It sounds corny, but my mum is my biggest inspiration. She is a strong-willed, funny and independent woman who is also the kindest most generous person I know.

Also, we are lucky that on the global stage we have plenty of inspiring women leaders right now – Nicola Sturgeon, Michelle Obama and Angela Merkel are my current favorites.

8. What advice would you give to your 16year old self?

Don't ever forget to look after yourself. Otherwise you will be no good to anyone else either. Remember the airplane safety code: put your own oxygen mask on before seeing to others who rely on you.

9. Your instant mindfulness fix...

Five minute meditation videos on YouTube – a great way to relax, refresh and restart when you are feeling stressed or tired.

10. And finally something frivolous: best thing about being a woman...

I don't know, it just feels right to me; women are amazing. Men are great too, but I would never want to have been born a man!

. . .

Top Takeaways from Emmajane:

- Build your confidence
- Put yourself forward, don't be constrained by barriers: Break down the barriers both external AND internal
- Being successful is an on-going objective — is not just achieving it, is maintaining it. Being successful is also satisfaction in a job well done
- Love what you do so it doesn't feel like work
- Have a good support work around you — the people you work with are important
- Meditation-a great way to relax, refresh and restart.

KAREN GREEN

K aren Green is a food mentor, business mentor, speaker, regular lecturer at Nottingham Trent University and author.

Her book **Recipe for Success** is aimed at foodpreneurs and MDs of SMEs food manufacturing businesses wanting to improve their business and grow it to the next level. It covers brand development, marketing, negotiation and so on.

Karen is also a foodie and judge for the "Great Taste Quality and Food Awards" and a woman who has turned her passion into a business as an entrepreneur.

Website:
   www.thefoodmentor.co.uk

1. When you were a child what was your dream job and why?

. . .

I really wanted to be a doctor when I grew up.

My father wanted me to be a bilingual secretary but I wanted something more glamorous.

My daughter is now at medical school as I found the science A levels too challenging and so went a business route instead.

2. Can you tell me the time that you started to consider yourself successful?

I was told by my line manager at Boots that I was rubbish and wouldn't amount to anything (I still have the appraisal) and then I was given a new manager and she mentored and developed me. I was promoted to buyer for Vitamins, which was the most coveted buyer's job in Boots, and I felt very proud and successful and after that I really flew.

3. I'm sure like every business/business person you have faced adversity: how do you motivate yourself and force through the worst times?

I have studied mental toughness and through that process have learnt many techniques for keeping going. My top three would be:

1. Great supportive network of friends and business mentors who keep me on the right road
2. My achievements log — every so often I do a log of what I have done that I am proud of so that I can take a quick read when it becomes a little bit challenging
3. Visualization and meditation techniques – I have learnt a few simple tricks for solving the immediate stresses e.g. pre important client meetings , etc.

4. What are the best things about your job?

I work with a variety of clients now on short and long term projects. The best thing is getting a new product launched on shelf — whether that is a small start up brand or an own label product that may have been two years in the making.

I also love mentoring people and seeing them grow from a personal point of view.

5. As Tony Robbins says, *"Success leaves clues"*: what are your daily/weekly habits?

- Sleep - I am early to bed, early to rise so try and keep to this routine and get as much sleep as possible
- Exercise - I get my best work done in the first hour of the day and then will do some form of exercise — either running or yoga. I live part of the time in France and need to get out early before it gets really hot
- Eating well – I love food but also love to ensure that I get a great balanced diet – I cannot function without regular meals
- Personal development – I am ALWAYS learning — at the moment, I am launching my book "Recipe for success" and so am learning about publishing, social media and book promotion techniques.

6. What do you think is the most significant barrier to female leadership?

One of the biggest issues for women is childcare — when a woman has her first baby, she can go back to work and the cost of childcare is less than her salary.

If she has a second baby, then that cost/benefit equation becomes more complicated. Some successful women have a husband who takes the strain but I do think that the interruption to a working career can be detrimental.

For me however, I have not really found this to be so much of a challenge but I only took four months for each of my children.

The other barrier other than the obvious male domination at the top and glass ceiling is in female heads. Termed the Imposter Syndrome, so many successful women I know deep down don't believe they should be there and so don't necessarily have the chutzpah to go for the big jobs.

I am sure there is some research, which shows that if women read a job ad they will apply if they have all the requirements and men if they have a third (or some such figure!).

7. What women inspire you and why?

Emma Jones at Enterprise Nation is a very strong character who does a great job for start-ups — she has been very helpful to me and is the best networker I know.

My mum — she was a stay at home mum until my dad died when I was 21 and then she got involved in saving Greenham common from being built on and ensured it went back to common land when the Americans left. In recognition of her work, Newbury designated a field and called it Audrey's meadow. Inspirational late developer!

8. What advice would you give to your 16year old self?

- Enjoy life and don't be in such a rush!!
- Believe in yourself, you are way better than you think
- Follow your dreams and don't let others talk you out of it.

9. Your instant mindfulness fix...

Concentrating on breathing — listening and feeling each breath coming in and out — easy to do anywhere and calming in about two minutes!

10. And finally something frivolous: best thing about being a woman...

Being able to flirt your way out of things!!

Top Takeaways from Karen

- Believe in yourself - You are way better than you think
- Keep an achievement log for when things get though
- Keep a supportive network of friends and business mentors to keep you on track
- Invest in your personal development - ALWAYS learn
- Enjoy life - Don't be in such a rush!

LIZ WARD

Liz Ward is Principal at **Virtuoso Legal**, the Award Winning IP Solicitors she set up in 2007 to deal with the specialist requirements of companies for intellectual property and information technology legal advice.

Liz has now led this field for ten years and continues to push the envelope with her work.

She is an expert in the healthcare and technology sectors (she has a 1st Degree in Genetics and Cell Biology and ten years+ healthcare business experience).

Liz also lectures and assists with electronic disclosure and theft of electronic information by employers and others.

Website:
www.virtuosolegal.com

. . .

1. When you were a child what was your dream job and why?

When I was a child I wanted to be a nurse and then a doctor.

I was influenced by my Mum who was a district nurse and midwife. I wanted to help people and I saw how satisfying that is from my Mum's work.

2. Can you tell me the time that you started to consider yourself successful?

I considered myself successful when I qualified as a lawyer. I'd completed the training as well as working doing another career and I then qualified into a big law firm at the time, which was a very difficult thing to achieve.

Lots of well-qualified and talented people never got jobs as trainees so they never got to become solicitors at all. Some of those who did didn't get a great training either so I knew how lucky I'd been to get to where I was.

3. I'm sure like every business/business person you have faced adversity: how do you motivate yourself and force through the worst times?

I'm really into mindset and keeping focused on a goal. It is easy to get distracted so I get my music on and go outside and do what is called my chain of excellence. Also like many people, I've had some major challenges, which always serve as useful reference points to call on for strength when the going gets tough.

· · ·

4. What are the best things about your job?

The variety and constant challenge of the law. I love helping people and putting £££ on their business! In fact, I just love business. It fascinates and stimulates me.

5. As Tony Robbins says, *"Success leaves clues"*: what are your daily/weekly habits?

My daily habits include walking and listening to music. I'm a big Tony Robbins fan! I'm also a fan of healthy eating, looking after your body, mind and soul. I'm an eternal optimist too which helps. Those are my daily habits although I do sometimes slip — especially when I'm not in my usual routine.

6. What do you think is the most significant barrier to female leadership?

The barriers are different for everyone but many women like to achieve balance rather than overall leadership, and so sacrifice career achievements in order to serve their families better.

You can have it all but generally not all at the same time! For many women their mindset shifts when they have children to think about. It is a natural phenomenon — why should we not be proud to put our children first? They're our legacy and their welfare is important for future generations. Leadership takes 100% commitment and so women are put off by it, as they know they can't or rather don't want to give 100% to one thing in their lives.

· · ·

7. What women inspire you and why?

I'm inspired by strong women such as Christine Lagarde, Benazir Bhutto, Sheryl Sandberg, Margaret Thatcher and Shirley Williams.

8. What advice would you give to your 16year old self?

You are beautiful — now get on with it and ignore the naysayers!

9. Your instant mindfulness fix...

Looking to the skies and saying a short prayer that starts with thank you Lord. Show me the way please.

10. And finally something frivolous: best thing about being a woman...

Clothes. Shoes. Handbags. Makeup!!
    Oh and sex. LOL.

Top Takeaways from Liz

- Leadership takes 100% commitment
- Keep focused on your goal — it is easy to get distracted
- Challenges serve as useful reference points to call on your strengths
- You are beautiful — now get on with it and ignore the naysayers!
- Look after your body, mind and soul.

ELA SLUTSKI & GALIT BAUER

Ela Sluski has business experience across Europe, the USA and Israel. She gained her first professional experience in Israel after graduating from Tel Aviv University.

Galit Bauer is Human Resources veteran with over 15 years experience in selecting and placing the right people in the right organizations. Galit moved to Amsterdam from Tel Aviv 15 years ago together with her husband Eilam and their Labrador Meshi.

Ela & Galit founded **Holiday Sitters** in 2016.

Holiday Sitters is an online babysitting platform designed especially for expats and tourists living in European destinations. Parents can book a babysitter they can trust according to availability, time and language. They can get to know the baby-sitters through moderated online profiles, video interviews and dedicated chat rooms.

Website:
    www.holiday-sitters.com

· · ·

1. When you were a child what was your dream job and why?

Ela: When I was a child I had a few dream jobs. I wanted to be a singer because I loved singing, and it seemed magical to be performing in front of a large audience.

I also wanted to be a doctor at some point, in order to help people. All the doctors I met looked like very smart people!

Galit: My dream job was to be a teacher.

I loved to stand in front of my imaginary class and talk, write stuff on the board and ask children questions.

I could stay busy for many hours with this, and always wanted to be a teacher who meant something to her students.

2 - Can you tell me the time that you started to consider yourself successful?

Ela: I moved to Israel when I was 19 year old, on my own, and I didn't know anyone and I didn't speak Hebrew. I had nothing, really. When I went to study in Tel Aviv University, whilst fully supporting myself financially, I considered myself successful.

Galit: As a student when I worked in 3 different jobs and lived by myself in Tel Aviv, I managed to be independent and not ask for any money from my parents. This was such a great feeling.

3 - I'm sure like every business/business person you have faced adversity: how do you motivate yourself and force through the worst times?

. . .

Ela: I think one of the things that helps me to deal with difficult times is to talk about it with my business partner and with my family, be open about it, and ask for support and advice.

Galit: I am a very optimistic person who trusts myself and my abilities, believing in hard work and commitment. I do a lot of sports, ask for hugs from my 8 year-old son, and listen to Les Brown - my favorite motivational speaker. Of course I have my husband who reminds me how much he loves me and believes in me.

4 - What are the best things about your job?

Ela: The best thing about my job is to wake up in the morning with a smile!

Galit: The freedom to make the decisions, the responsibility for your own destiny, and the creation of something new and unique. I love to make people happy with the product, whilst working with the great and inspirational people around me. There's a happiness that you don't need to report to a useless manager, too.

5 - As Tony Robbins says, "Success leaves clues": what are your daily/weekly habits?

Ela: I check my emails and messages in the morning and if there is nothing really urgent that requires my immediate attention, I have a moment with my kids and take them to school.

It's important for me to spend time with them, and it gives me energy. Afterwards I bike to work through the canals of Amsterdam. Even on a rainy day, I still feel privileged to be able to do that.

Then it's a regular day in the office with tasks, emails, and other things that need to be done.

Galit: Sport, breathing, Yoga, listening to Les Brown, talking on a weekly basis with our mentor, and every Friday evening investing time with my family — plus a winner mindset!

6 - What do you think is the most significant barrier to female leadership?

Ela: I think there's no barrier to the female leadership.

Rather, I think there are a lot of barriers to leadership in general. The most significant one is to manage to stay a decent person.

Galit: Sometimes it's us women who do not believe that a female can lead — this is the most significant barrier to us.

We have self doubt and unfortunately it's also supported by society.

7 - What women inspire you and why?

Ela: I admire single mothers, I think it's an extremely hard job — rewarding but hard. It requires so much from the person and if you look at the "job requirements" these are the skills you need in order to be successful in everything

Galit: Women who don't ask "Is it OK?". Women who dare to say what they WANT and feel free to be STRONG.

8 - What advice would you give to your 16 year old self?

. . .

Ela: Not to worry about what other people think and say, stay true to yourself and do not be afraid to dream, because they will come true if you really want them to.

Galit: Travel all the time and travel the world as long as you can.

9 - Your instant mindfulness fix...

Ela: Go outside for a few minutes if weather allows, or just take a moment and dive into my own world.

Galit: No other choice but to WIN continue dreaming and visualize the success.

10 - And finally something frivolous: best thing about being a woman...

Ela: Everything really; motherhood, being super emotional about my kids, being unconditionally in love, to know how to love, being a family, starting a business, having a girls night out, and having more than three pairs of shoes and being able to love each and every one equally!

There's much more, of course!

Galit: Accepting NO it is not an option, the ability to do few things together at the same time, and the last and the most amazing is for your child to say to you "I love you Mama".

. . .

Top Takeaways from Ela & Galit

• In difficult times be open about it — ask for support and advice

• Talk to your Mentor on a regular basis & invest time with your family

• Trust yourself and your abilities

• Don't worry what other people think: stay true to yourself and don't be afraid to dream big

• Visualize your dreams.

ELENA KALE

E lena Kale is the Founder of **Inspired Marketing Media** delivering bespoke marketing services tailored to customer needs.

Elena is a Senior Leadership team/boardroom level sales, marketing and events professional with more than 20 years experience of developing strategy and driving customer engagement across a variety of different sectors.

Elena was previously Divisional Director for the KCS Group and Group Commercial Manager at Snozone Ltd.

Website:
www.inspiredmarketingmedia.co.uk

1. When you were a child what was your dream job and why?

I wanted to be a fashion designer as a younger child, I was always drawing and being creative; as I became a teenager I loved writing fiction and was going to do an English degree until my A-level results said otherwise and I selected business studies. It was the right decision but I still feel there's a book inside me and I've written copy & content throughout my career.

2. Can you tell me the time that you started to consider yourself successful?

I'm my own worst critic so I'm always driving myself to be better however during my corporate life I set up a group sales & events subsidiary division from scratch which ended up being very successful and is still in operation today. It's an achievement I'm proud of but I could not have done it without some amazing people that I worked with throughout the years.

Within the same company I was also promoted to the executive leadership team in 2012, meaning I'd reached the highest point I could and was involved in shaping the strategy and direction of the business.

However I've learnt through being self-employed to celebrate the small successes as well as the larger ones; getting referrals out of the blue, learning to network and speak publicly without feeling terrified and rebuilding my income back to corporate levels through getting out of my comfort zone.

3. I'm sure like every business/business person you have faced adversity: how do you motivate yourself and force through the worst times?

I've been alive long enough to know that life has its ups and its downs, some very extreme, but that nothing stays exactly the same. You're always moving forward and when you go through a tough time as long as you're proactive and working towards your goals you will have a break-through. Sometimes life takes you to the wire before you get that break but if you stay positive, visualize what you want as if you have it already and keep working, it will come.

It's also important to ask for help when you need it. We cannot be great at everything, we all have our own key skills and you can waste more time trying to fix something than if you had asked an expert. Time is precious, it's the one thing we can't buy, but it does cost.

4. What are the best things about your job?

Working for yourself provides a huge amount of flexibility so I'm more able to work around my children and other things I need to do in my personal life.

It is quite satisfying not having to ask permission to book holiday on certain dates!

I can also plan my week around key appointments or events i.e. school sports days but also to suit the way that I work. I know my most productive times of the day so I focus specific activities at those times.

I can also choose to work over 7 days if I want to do shorter week days — it's good to take time off too so I don't do this every week.

I also know that my "destiny" is down to me — if I want to make more money I need to work harder and work smarter.

Opportunities are all around us and as I'm my own boss I'm free to pursue those that I feel would be the best for my business.

· · ·

5. As Tony Robbins says, *"Success leaves clues"*: what are your daily/weekly habits?

I have a planner/journal that I use regularly for both business and personal meetings and things to do which have a week across both pages so it's easy to see what I'm doing!

This helps me plan out set projects and retained hours by breaking down what work is needed in order to meet deadlines. I also look at it each night so I pre-plan for the following day.

I use social media a lot although I need to use it more for my business; I have a Hootsuite account so will be going back to this to schedule posts a week ahead.

I write to-do lists although I try to keep them as short and concise as possible to stop feeling overwhelmed.

I also try to prioritize tasks at certain times where they fit into my productivity and way of working, for example I'm better at tackling certain things in the morning, other more admin based items I may leave until the evenings or weekends.

6. What do you think is the most significant barrier to female leadership?

In corporate life it's still a man's world and without sounding like a staunch feminist until the pay gap is properly addressed and fathers start taking extended paternity leave the issue of motherhood will always affect our careers.

. . .

Becoming a mum made me realize the qualities and lessons you learn whilst bringing up a mini-me, makes parents better rather than worse employees — time & conflict management, negotiation skills, planning and sheer resilience are key within business.

Women bring a different perspective to the boardroom, yes it can be a softer, more humanitarian approach — although no female board member got there without a backbone of steel — but she gives balance. Men need to be taught as little boys that women are equals both at home and in work but this will take decades.

The rise in mumpreneurs and female business owners is no surprise as it gives us more flexibility and the chance to try and juggle more effectively.

In our own business we are the leaders but our own female lack of self-confidence can also hold us back — are we good enough, can we make it work?

Ask a male entrepreneur and he knows 100% yes, women in general, over analyze and take things very personally which ends up with anxiety and worrying about something that may never happen.

Until flexible working becomes normality — for everyone not just parents — and respect that becoming a mum does not stop you from wanting a career or still being damn good at it — the rise of female leaders will be primarily through their own entrepreneurial skills.

But, we also need to learn to lift each other up, not compete against each other.

. . .

7. What women inspire you and why?

My grandmother, who sadly passed away many years ago, opened a home furnishings shop on the day the second world war broke out yet she still made it a great success during those years and beyond.

She had a natural sales ability, which she passed to my mum; both easily connect(ed) with people on an emotional level who became customers almost without realizing it!

Regardless of political beliefs Margaret Thatcher was still the first female prime minister and negotiated hard in a world that was even more male dominated than it is today.

One of my best friends worked tirelessly and against the odds to become a pilot over 24 years ago after she was laughed at by the school's careers adviser.

She's still flying today, now alongside more female pilots than when she trained and every time I look inside a plane's cockpit I feel immensely proud of what she achieved.

8. What advice would you give to your 16year old self?

Believe in yourself and don't be afraid to reach further out of your comfort zone.

Also worrying is like praying for something bad to happen — we all worry at times but it's rarely as bad as you think it's going to be. It just holds you back.

. . .

9. Your instant mindfulness fix...

Gratitude – it's easy as a solo-preneur to worry about growth or where the next piece of work is coming from but it's important to reflect on what you have achieved and be grateful for the small successes as these lead to bigger ones.

I try to keep a positive outlook on life in general as well.

I also find beaches very inspirational – I could sit on a beach and stare at the waves for hours, preferably somewhere hot!

We all have a "happy place" and sometimes just having an image of a beach in my office helps me to refocus and also helps with my creativity. It's why I use images of beaches as part of my branding.

10. And finally something frivolous: best thing about being a woman...

The fact that we can dress far more creatively and flamboyantly than men; nails, make up, hair, color — need I say more!

Women tend to be more intuitive and I love the fact that if you get a bunch of women together and they can very quickly bond and forge long lasting connections.

Whilst childbirth itself is hideous, having two girls of my own made me respect what women's bodies are capable of and the amazing way that mother nature works — it's not called "Mother" nature for nothing.

· · ·

Top Takeaways from Elena

- Your destiny is down to you
- Believe in yourself and don't be afraid to reach beyond your comfort zone
- Opportunities are all around us: pursue those that feel best for you
- Prioritize tasks around your own productivity and way of working
- Find your "happy place" and keep images to remind you and refocus.

KATIE OWEN

Katie Owen is the Founder of **Sargasso & Grey**, a luxury British shoe brand that launched in 2014, designing and producing luxury shoes and stilettos for women who require shoes in a more spacious fit but still expect them to be stylish and attractive.

This exciting shoe brand is making a name for itself challenging the view that wide fit shoes cannot be comfortable and beautiful.

Katie found out that her feet got wider after the birth off her first child (a common but permanent side effect of pregnancy) and decided to create a brand to cater for women who like wearing stylish shoes and heels bye need a wider fit.

Website:
   www.sargassoandgrey.com

1. When you were a child what was your dream job and why?

I must confess to having lots of dream jobs when I was a child. Firstly it was a vet and then an actress, before eventually settling on a pilot. I ended up working in banking. I am not sure what happened! Perhaps now running a shoe business, where I get to design beautiful shoes alongside my "day job" is my way of bringing out the creativity in me!

2. Can you tell me the time that you started to consider yourself successful?

I guess it depends how you define "success".

There are certain achievements I have made as part of building my shoe business that I would deem a "success". Setting up a company from scratch. Establishing a brand. Putting in place a production line. Selling shoes. Lorraine Kelly where a pair on her breakfast show. Featuring in Prima Magazine. Getting amazing feedback from lovely customers. Seeing repeat orders come in.

Success shouldn't be measured by the end game as there are lots of successes on the way, as well as many failures, and whilst it is important not to lose sight of the ultimate goal, whatever that may be, it is also hugely important to recognize the smaller but significant individual successes on the journey.

3. I'm sure like every business/business person you have faced adversity: how do you motivate yourself and force through the worst times?

Sometimes things go wrong, or at least don't go as planned.

. . .

Whether it is orders from the shoe factory not arriving on time, shoes returned (perhaps they didn't fit or weren't the right color) or getting stressed out by competitors, there can be so many distractions reasons to feel down and de-motivated.

The key thing is to keep going and just take each day as it comes. If you are certain you have a great product/idea/service persevere and use the stumbling blocks as stepping-stones.

4. What are the best things about your job?

Without a doubt it is happy customers.

I absolutely love it when customers email me to say they love the shoes. It is all the more special because usually they have searched high and low to find the perfect pair of wide fit shoes so they are especially delighted!

5. As Tony Robbins says, *"Success leaves clues"*: what are your daily/weekly habits?

My business is small but growing, so much of the day-to-day activity is all down to me, as well as working in my day job of banking.

That said, I recognize the things that I can do well (the customer service side, the shoe design, supply side) and where I lack the knowledge or experience (web design, SEO) I get the experts in.

. . .

6. What do you think is the most significant barrier to female leadership?

I think women struggle to effectively delegate. That is why they are so busy and often take on too much. I definitely see this trait in myself. Maybe it's about not letting go of control, but to run a successful business you have to focus on what you are good at and delegate the areas where you are not as strong.

Confidence is also something a lot of women lack: confidence and self-belief.

For ages I called my business my "expensive hobby". I was running it alongside my day job, it was all self funded, I reduced my employed hours to devote time to it, so had to take a pay cut and I was scared of it not being "successful," so I belittled my efforts.

Then a male friend said to me "if *you* don't take your business seriously, no one else will". That was a real turning point for me.

7. What women inspire you and why?

There are so many women who inspire me: successful entrepreneurs, full time mums; mums with careers. Women who volunteer or spend their life helping others.

Inspirational women are the ones who are positive and supportive of other women.... And don't judge!

. . .

8. What advice would you give to your 16year old self?

Explore life more. Don't be confined to following the well-trodden path. Make your mistakes early and learn from them. Try new things. Be confident. Be kind.

9. Your instant mindfulness fix…

When things seem overwhelming, think of the most stressful things that you felt happened to you in the last 10 years. How do you feel about them now?

Hopefully the answer is that they are insignificant. In which case, soon so will this current "major drama"!

10. And finally something frivolous: best thing about being a woman…

Now is a great time to be a woman. We are pushing forward with equal pay and there are lots of arenas for women in business to come together and support each other and share experiences.

Women now feel empowered to be able to achieve their ambitions as well as having a family. The two are not mutually exclusive.

There are few limitations and lots of opportunities, as proved by the fact that our PM is female, as is the leader of the Scottish Parliament and the Scottish Conservative party.

And if that wasn't good enough, we don't have to shave our faces every day either!

. . .

Top Takeaways from Katie

- Recognize the smaller but significant individual successes along the way — not just the end game
- No matter what, keep going and take each day as it comes
- Get the experts in where you lack the knowledge overall and focus on what you are good at
- Take your business/career seriously — if you don't, no one else will
- Explore life, try new things, and be kind.

SOPHIE THORNE

S ophie Thorne is a serial entrepreneur and business strategist.
She helps female service-based entrepreneurs shift from solo-preneur to CEO.

The Growth Edit is her signature 90 day program.

Prior to working as a business strategist, Sophie was the Founder and CEO of Twisted Lingerie, a lingerie company aimed at empowering women in their sexuality.

Website:
www.sophiethorne.co.uk

1. When you were a child what was your dream job and why?

To be honest, I can't remember having a dream job as a child. I remember telling my future secondary school headmistress that I wanted to be a hairdresser in an interview but I also wanted to be a florist, photographer, model, teacher, magazine editor, lawyer, fashion designer...I was clearly very indecisive as a child!

. . .

2. Can you tell me the time that you started to consider yourself successful?

Launching my businesses.

The journey, for example, to get Twisted Lingerie from my initial idea to launch was scary and, since my background isn't in lingerie (or even in fashion), a steep learning curve and a lot of hard work. Reaching that point made me feel like I had achieved something I could be proud of — regardless of what the future held!

3. I'm sure like every business/business person you have faced adversity: how do you motivate yourself and force through the worst times?

There were so many challenges — a never-ending stream of challenges — when I was launching my business but I was persistent, dedicated, optimistic and patient.

There were many moments when I could have just given up but I pushed myself because I really believed in what I was building.

Starting a business is ridiculously hard and takes a huge amount of dedication, late nights, weekends and many, many compromises.

One thing I've realized is that if you're not passionate about the business you're building, you'll feel really burdened by the work.

. . .

4. What are the best things about your job?

Running my own business means that the terms are entirely my own, and — frankly — nothing is better than that.

5. As Tony Robbins says, *"Success leaves clues"*: what are your daily/weekly habits?

About five years ago I read a Vanity Fair article about Barack Obama. In it he explains that he only wears blue or grey suits because he doesn't want to waste time making decisions about what he's wearing when he has so many other decisions to make.

The concept really resonated — having a fixed routine means I'm able to be more productive as I don't get distracted by trivial things; for example, I decide what I'm going to wear and eat the following day before I go to bed, I only socialize (be it for business or pleasure) once in the workweek, and if something comes up that isn't on my to do, I won't do it (at least not that day).

6. What do you think is the most significant barrier to female leadership?

There's no right way to answer this question. I'm very aware (and have unfortunately been on the receiving end) of the huge amount of bias that exists for women in business but — in many respects – I think the most significant barrier to female leadership is yourself.

As Sheryl Sandberg explains so well in her book "Lean In," women (unintentionally) hold themselves back and this prevents them from achieving their full potential, including the leadership positions they are more than capable of having.

7. What women inspire you and why?

I'm constantly inspired by and in awe of the many women around me — from the stay-at-home mums trying to do a million things at once and the working mothers who manage to find time for everything to the women who work 60+ hour weeks and the ladies who are somehow able to fit vast amounts of charity work round all their other commitments.

I see many daily examples, which inspire me to be a better person in all areas of my life.

8. What advice would you give to your 16year old self?

That it's ok to make mistakes; everything you do doesn't have to be perfect (I would probably benefit from telling my 30-year-old self the same thing!).

9. Your instant mindfulness fix...

Working out — exercise always clears my head.

10. And finally something frivolous: best thing about being a woman...

The lingerie.

. . .

Top Takeaways from Sophie

- The most significant barrier to women in leadership is themselves – Don't hold yourself back
- There are always challenges: push yourself and believe
- Nothing is better than living on your own terms
- It is ok to make mistakes — everything doesn't need to be perfect
- Have a fixed routine to be more productive — focus on the real decisions rather than the small things.

ALEXANDRA WALL

Alexandra Wall is the Founder of the Cardiff based label **Xandra Jane**, which she set up at the age of 23, offering a fresh twist on the fashion industry.

Sustainable, contemporary and rebellious, the award nominated **Xandra Jane** explores gender neutral clothing through zero waste processes and up cycled luxury, reconnecting you to your clothing and rebelling against fast fashion.

Website:
www.xandrajanedesign.com

1. When you were a child what was your dream job and why?

I had a handful, ranging from being an author to mounted police. Mounted police was short-lived, I just wanted to ride the horses, I didn't realize you had to serve as a normal officer for two years first. I could never settle my mind on one thing but I knew I wanted to be my own boss and I've always been creative, before attending university it was a split decision between choreography and fashion. How different things could have been!

2. Can you tell me the time that you started to consider yourself successful?

The definition of success is subjective; mine was when I became truly happy in what I do for a living. I was 23 when I established Xandra Jane, to be financially independent is a massive task in life, to be truly happy alongside that seems near impossible, but I've done it, and I've done it all by myself at a very young age, with no business partner and without borrowing a penny. How can I ask for anything more?

3. I'm sure like every business/business person you have faced adversity: how do you motivate yourself and force through the worst times?

To be vulnerably honest, I lost my mum when I was 19 years old; she suffered a long battle with MS and died at 56 years of age. When things get stressful within the fashion industry, as they often do, I remind myself they're just clothes and this really isn't the worst day of my life. Growing up with such a strong inspirational female figure I'm extremely grateful for being able to do the smallest things, so I make the small stuff count and it naturally feeds into bigger effects.

4. What are the best things about your job?

No two days are the same. I wrote a blog post recently about The Day In the Life of a Fashion Designer, and it was incredibly difficult to generalize everything into one generic day.

• • •

My entire purpose revolves around creating something new or seeing things from a different perspective. My job is to continually expand my learning and knowledge of my craft; it's very absorbing in the best possible way. I also love that I can exercise the morals and ethics I care so strongly about, the ones which are sadly lacking in the industry in the grand scheme of things, but businesses like mine are driving change, and it's incredible to be a part of that movement.

5. As Tony Robbins says, *"Success leaves clues"*: what are your daily/weekly habits?

Get. Up. Early. I'm talking no later than 06:00 am. My partner is a farmer so he arises at 04:30 am every morning. I can't say I spring out of bed but my productivity is at its highest in the first half of the day, you also harness the time to its full potential when you wake up early.

Exercise and take care of yourself, if you start to crumble in health, your business will follow. Take that half an hour to hit the gym or get some fresh air, to disconnect from work, drink lots of water — it honestly energizes you like you wouldn't believe and eat healthy though don't obsessively restrict yourself, food can often lift my mood in an instant!

Making time for friends and family also comes into health and wellbeing, it can be hard to overlook this when establishing a business as you know they will always be there for you, but that shouldn't matter, you should still invest your love into the people that give it back.

Business related habits: I schedule social media once a week, usually on a Sunday, although I organically post throughout the week, I am still maintaining a presence online should work overwhelm me at any point to forget.

. . .

Post frequently. If you write a blog, schedule as far in advance as needed. Once every two months I will often sit down for the day and churn out posts I have been inspired to write over time. It's integral for me to write my blog posts to connect with my customer and build rapport, proving there is a human behind the brand.

6. What do you think is the most significant barrier to female leadership?

Support and communication.

Admitting to any mistakes often leads to respect, we often feel as though being a woman already sets us off on weaker footing, and so we must portray strength and perfection. But perfection doesn't exist and we are stronger in numbers. I still take the bins out in my world and wouldn't ask an employee or intern to do anything I wouldn't do myself. Lead by example and conduct yourself with honesty.

7. What women inspire you and why?

Women who work hard for what they want, whether that's a family in which they stay at home and nurture their children, or to independently go traveling; ambition is a personal journey, and you have to respect and admire anyone who achieves their goals.

I think it can be easy to "settle," settle for that job that pays the bills but doesn't fulfill your life, settle for the town you grew up in without seeing the world like you so wanted to do — hats off to the women who take risks even if they don't pay off, because the energy they display to do something so brave can only be commended.

· · ·

8. What advice would you give to your 16year old self?

Spend time with loved ones and don't take them for granted. Support others on their own journey and success because you are the only person in charge of yours, don't sweat the small stuff and persevere — apply yourself to everything you do and don't be afraid to try new things.

9. Your instant mindfulness fix...

I have always struggled with "emptying my mind" and so I dedicate at least 10 minutes a day to sketching, I not only find this a form of meditation as it focuses my energy on something unrelated and therapeutic, but it increases my skill in visual communication which is critical for my career path and my job in particular. Being able to lose myself on something as simple as an A4 page is very humbling and detracts from the buzz of modern day technology.

10. And finally something frivolous: best thing about being a woman...

The liberation to be whatever I want, the balance of sensitivity and strength which drives forward independence, ambition and the ability to achieve against all odds with emotional resilience of the spirit. Society's ideologies allow me to be sympathetic and resistant at the same time without pressure to be confused by my emotions.

I hope the balance comes for men. I am not pressured to be a breadwinner, nor do I have to provide children – I can choose my own path (in this country) and my destiny is in my hands. I am very lucky to be a woman.

. . .

Top Takeaways from Alexandra

- Be happy in what you do for a living
- Make the small stuff count and be grateful
- Take care of yourself: if your health crumbles, your business will follow
- Make time for friends and family and to disconnect
- Don't settle.

JULIE BISHOP

J ulie Bishop is the founder of **Jobhop**, the site where employers and candidates socially connect.

Julie is passionate about showing companies how to attract and retain talent, as well as showing job seekers how to market themselves to improve career opportunities.

She is the author of **The Social Jobseeker** as well as a writer for Glassdoor; her articles have regularly been featured in Forbes, CNBC and The Independent.

Julie is also a public speaker on topics such as social recruiting , the future workplace and digital natives.

Additionally she delivers training for companies who seek to improve their brand and company culture.

Website:
  www.jobhop.co.uk

• • •

1. When you were a child what was your dream job and why?

When I was young, I can't ever remember wanting a job.

What I do remember is wanting to be famous, however, a much wiser person told me all about the complications of being famous, which completely put me off. I then decided that I would just try to be the best at whatever it is I do. I was only ten; everything seemed easy then!

2. Can you tell me the time that you started to consider yourself successful?

I've never considered myself successful, but other people tell me I am so I must be just critical.

3. I'm sure like every business/business person you have faced adversity: how do you motivate yourself and force through the worst times?

There's always a solution, but sometimes you're so involved that you don't see it.

When things get tough, I take time out, which sounds like I'm running away, but it's not. I will go for a sauna, or a walk by the beach, anywhere which is quiet and away from the business.

I completely switch off and recharge. After a while, new thoughts start to come into my head, and by the time I get back to business I'm recharged, motivated and have the solution, it always works.

. . .

4. What are the best things about your job?

I love everything about Jobhop, but I think the best bit is finding the perfect candidate for an employer in a matter of no time when they've tried every other method and have given up hope.

5. As Tony Robbins says, "*Success leaves clues*": what are your daily/weekly habits?

So, what do I do that is hard to give up?

Every day I seek new information on technology advancements because I always want to be one step ahead and prepared.

I walk my dog a couple of times every day because it's good for both of us. I go to the gym at least five times a week because I want to be strong and healthy, it must work because I'm never off ill.

I also have a spoonful of local honey every day; it's supposed to be good for you. If I was asked to stop any of those, I think I would have withdrawal symptoms.

6. What do you think is the most significant barrier to female leadership?

I don't believe there are any barriers to female leadership.

It's about the desire for it, the sacrifices, the hustle, kicking down doors and understanding that "No" means maybe.

· · ·

7. What women inspire you and why?

Valentina Tereshkova.

It was 1963, and she became the first woman in space at the age of 26. Valentina was a textile worker who had big dreams, she kept them to herself though because female textile workers don't become astronauts, or that's what everyone else thought! When it was time for her to go up into space, she told her parents she was going skydiving.

8. What advice would you give to your 16year old self?

Don't laugh at the mobile phone it will get smaller, just ask for Vodafone shares for your Birthday.

9. Your instant mindfulness fix...

Do something that makes you live in the moment. For example, I horse ride, and when I'm on a horse I don't think about what happened yesterday or what could happen tomorrow, all I concentrate on is staying on the horse.

You have to enjoy the now, but when you're wrapped up in business constantly planning for the next six months and analyzing what happened over the past six months, it can be hard. That's why it's good to find something where you have to concentrate on the now and nothing else.

10. And finally something frivolous: best thing about being a woman...

The best thing about being a woman apart from shoes is the ability to give birth to another human being. For me it's my son who's now 18, he's my best friend and is a great help with Jobhop, always bringing his youthful energy to it.

Top Takeaways from Julie

- Try to be the best at whatever it is you do
- Keep your dreams to yourself if you are surrounded by skeptics — just keep going
- Understand that "NO" means maybe – Kick that door & hustle
- When things get though, take time out — there is always a solution
- Do something that makes you live in the moment – Enjoy the Now!

KIRSTEN REES

Kirsten Rees is a Copyrighter, Business Coach, Published Author and Founder of **MakeMeASuccess**, an haute copy & couture coaching company producing purposeful content that feels authentic and attracts customers.

Website:
   www.makemeasuccess.co.uk

1. When you were a child what was your dream job and why?

I wanted to be a primary school teacher. I think it was a comfort thing as I was rather an awkward, painfully shy girl and school was an environment I already knew.

Although I loved scribbling stories, no one ever inspired the idea that anything creative like writing or art could be taken seriously as a career. Instead, I was encouraged to go to college and qualify as something practical. I had normal, working-class parents and no female role models in my life who were self-employed.

In a way, I have become a teacher of sorts and on a bigger platform as I launched my own business as a copywriter and business coach helping female entrepreneurs find their voice. I'm also a published author, which I hope will stimulate at least a few minds in the next generation.

2. Can you tell me the time that you started to consider yourself successful?

I think it was probably when I was financially able to take time out from my career running my copywriting business to write and publish my debut novel. I'm now working on a second book, and it's an incredible thing to be able to have two careers that you enjoy.

For my own writing, I often take myself away up north in Scotland on writing trips. If I feel like not working on a Monday and going to a spa, or for a walk to really relax and get creative, then I can do that because I manage my own schedule.

With my company MakeMeASuccess, I'm very much a hugs not handshakes kind of woman in business. I'm established enough that I was able to carve out my own brand so I wear dresses I like or jeans if I feel like it rather than smart suits.

I offer Wine & Whine coaching sessions because I want to work with women like myself who enjoy a glass of vino while we troubleshoot their business problems. Having the confidence to do these things comes from experience of doing this more than five years and the incredible feedback I get from my clients.

. . .

3. I'm sure like every business/business person you have faced adversity: how do you motivate yourself and force through the worst times?

Yes, there have been more than a few moments of self-doubt and doubt cast by friends and family albeit less from them as I'm very conscientious about keeping positive, supportive people in my life.

I actually have a vision board and put things on it that I want, everything from the odd material possession, places I want to visit, things I'd love to try. However, it's mainly achievements I want like sitting on the couch on Ellen one day, meeting some of my writing heroes, having my book series published and made into a movie. It ranges from small to huge dreams and those keep me motivated!

4. What are the best things about your job?

I finally feel like I get to be myself every day! I'm not putting on a suit or uniform, smiling because someone tells me, or working my butt off for someone else's dream. I'm creating a path for myself and ticking off a bucket list of my own dreams.

I get to help amazing, passionate entrepreneurs discover their voice in selling without sounding "salesy". Every day is different; I could be meeting a client to discuss their website content, having a Skype chat with an international client, I might be editing a client's book, or being flown down to London for a photo-shoot and interview.

. . .

And in between all that I make time to unleash my creative imagination writing about magic and mystical creatures for my YA fantasy book series Forever Gone.

5. As Tony Robbins says, *"Success leaves clues"*: what are your daily/weekly habits?

Absolutely! There's no perfect path to success that will work for everyone. Sometimes, you need to learn the hard way, but there are also talented and experienced people out there you can learn from. So I follow those who are five, ten, twenty years ahead of me instead of watching my competitors.

I have a diary where I schedule in working hours, marketing hours, networking hours, and even downtime. I plan ahead when it comes to events and strategies for publicity.

I have a proper alarm clock and not a phone alarm to make sure I get up because I'm not a morning person. I use a great app called Headspace if I'm feeling out of sorts and make time for exercise to keep myself healthy mentally and physically.

My biggest learning curve has been that you don't need to wait until you're a success to start talking about yourself and your business, nominating yourself for awards, or getting publicity. You can do it all in year one!

6. What do you think is the most significant barrier to female leadership?

. . .

I think we're often our own barriers in our careers whether it's confidence, not supporting one another, or a lack of education in the bigger picture. Women don't need permission or a hand up to be equal with men although we do need their support. We can launch our own businesses and hire other great women, vote for better political candidates who have equality at the forefront of their education and economic policies, and give time to the generation who follow us.

We can make things happen and bring about change now and for our future. I've been back to my old high school to talk with students on a careers evening. I still offer complimentary advice and installment plans for startups, even though I have bigger clients. I've done over 200hours volunteer work with a charity because I want to give back. I know if we all paid it forward more often, we would all benefit in the long run.

7. What women inspire you and why?

My mother firstly, because she always tried to fix things and just wanted life to be better and easier for us. My brother and I grew up always encouraged to think "what if" and it's given me a belief in the impossible when it comes to writing.

Secondly, I'm part of Natalie MacNeil's Conquer Club, and I love the community spirit amongst the women who are part of it. Then there are women who did great things before their time like Amelia Earhart, Emmeline Pankhurst, Rosa Parks, the Bronte sisters, and the list goes on.

8. What advice would you give to your 16year old self?

The things you dislike about yourself are going to become your greatest assets. One day, you'll love that you were an introvert because it meant you were in your own head so much and your mind is such an incredible tool.

You'll be grateful for the fears you had because it made you face them eventually one by one. If you stop believing what you think other people think of you, you'll discover you're very much loved by some wonderful people.

9. Your instant mindfulness fix...

I have an image on my phone that reads, "Stop doing shit you hate. Love your body more. Hang with awesome peeps. Smash some goals. Walk barefoot. Share your magic. Be freaking brave. Flaunt your awesome. Love harder & love louder. Be kinder to yourself. Be a nice human being. Give assholes the boot".

I'm not sure who created this but I love it and it's a daily reminder to let go of negativity and find the silver linings in everything. I always say to my clients even the worst or silliest writing can inspire something great, do you think Shakespeare got Romeo & Juliet right on the first draft? In the words of Cinderella in the new Disney movie "have courage and be kind".

10. And finally something frivolous: best thing about being a woman...

The support and community spirit amongst women in business and writing is amazing. I've been invited to great events because of a quick conversation and even ended up with new clients because my beautiful coat sparked a compliment from another woman and we got chatting!

. . .

I have an incredible and rather large family, and the women, in particular, are very close and often meet for cake and a catch-up.

I grew up surrounded by women who have survived a lot in life, women who haven't asked for much, who never get enough credit, but who genuinely love and support one another.

They are the ones who inspired me to volunteer as a Teen Mentor, who encouraged me to go traveling in my twenties, to write down my stories and share them, and who picked me up whenever I was down. I wouldn't be who or where I am without other women.

Top Takeaways from Kirsten

- Keep positive and supportive people in your life
- Create a path for yourself and tick off your own bucket list of dreams
- There is no perfect path to success that works for everyone — find your own way but keep on learning
- You can make things happen and bring about change now and for the future — the change that you want
- Let go of negativity and find a silver lining in everything.

CHERYL LUZET

C heryl Luzet is the Founder and Director of the website optimization agency **Wagada**.

Wagada specialties are:
usability, accessibility, search engine optimization, web building, project management, copy-editing and copy-writing.

Cheryl is a specialist on the online world with 15 plus years experience managing, editing and optimizing websites, gaining her experience in the website optimization world working in a variety of industries including travel, the NHS and educational publishing.

Cheryl has a Master's degree in Electronic Publishing from City University.

Website:
www.wagada.co.uk

. . .

1. When you were a child what was your dream job and why?

I wanted to be an archaeologist as I was fascinated by carbon dating. I'm glad I didn't do that job as the practicality of working away from home, outdoors in a muddy field, searching for a needle in a haystack wouldn't have agreed with me at all!

2. Can you tell me the time that you started to consider yourself successful?

I think being successful is all-relative. We are all successful in our own way, as no one really knows what challenges others are facing. For me success has been about employing enough staff to create a positive atmosphere at the Christmas party.

When we were just 3 or 4 staff, it was quite tricky to create the right environment for a staff outing, particularly as we have quite a range of ages. When we got to the point of 8 or 9 staff, everyone had someone that they got on really well with and could spend the evening with. It is a lovely thing to see everyone enjoying themselves!

3. I'm sure like every business/business person you have faced adversity: how do you motivate yourself and force through the worst times?

I am an eternal optimist! I have worked some very long hours running my business. I have young children and it is important that I am around for them, so every evening after they are in bed I get back to work until late.

.   .   .

Things are better now but there have been periods where I haven't sat and relaxed on the sofa for 8 or 9 months at a time. But every day I would say to myself — tomorrow is another day and will be better!

4. What are the best things about your job?

The flexibility to be available for my family has been the best thing about running my own business, and being local so I can pop to a school event and then back to the office easily. I needed to work but it was really important to me to be available for my family.

Because of this it has always been really important to me that my staff also benefit from being able to work flexibly.

Quite a few of my staff are also mums so I have been able to offer them part-time working, flexible hours and working from home. No one needs to miss sports day or the school Christmas play — these things are so important.

5. As Tony Robbins says, *"Success leaves clues"*: what are your daily/weekly habits?

Outsourcing has been the key to getting everything done in as few hours as possible so I can spend time with my family.

I find that my email is the thing that takes up the vast majority of my time, so I have a virtual assistant who tidies and organizes my email for me.

I have built up a team who all have different roles and support the business — from bookkeeping to purchasing a new kettle.

. . .

6. What do you think is the most significant barrier to female leadership?

I believe confidence is an issue. Men have a very different way of communicating to women and sometimes women can feel excluded.

7. What women inspire you and why?

Sheryl Sandberg is a really strong character and I admire the way that she has stood up for herself. Her book is inspirational and she offers really strong practical advice about being a mum and working in business.

I love JK Rowling more and more as I follow her on Twitter. She didn't let her situation prevent her from achieving great things, but also hasn't let success go to her head.

Here is a woman who has morals and will put herself on the line to stand up for what she believes in.

She has kept a strong head even though she has gained substantial wealth.

An awesome role model!

8. What advice would you give to your 16year old self?

Don't be in such a hurry to start being a grown up. And remember that my destiny is to work for myself. I was a terrible employee and completely naïve to the politics that seem to be obligatory in organizations large and small. I fell into running my business after my second child so it almost didn't happen — but I am so glad that did.

9. Your instant mindfulness fix...

I breathe out really deeply and it seems to ground me. Also I have read Amy Cuddy's book "Presence" that talks about using body language to make yourself feel more confident — the Starfish move always does the trick for me!

10. And finally something frivolous: best thing about being a woman...

The relationships that women can build up over a gin — we can be silly and have a laugh and still achieve great things.

Top Takeaways from Cheryl

- Define what success means to you
- Tomorrow is another day and will be better
- Don't let your situation prevent you from achieving great things
- Outsourcing is a great tool for entrepreneurs/small-biz
- Breathe.

IRINA BRAGIN

I rina Bragin is the Founder of **Made of Carpet**, carpet bags, trendy renaissance fashion treasure, straight from its homeland - London, England.

The idea for these beautiful unique bags was inspired by the romantic Victorian Era and influenced by famous English literary characters like Mary Poppins and Miss Marple.

The bags are made from the finest quality rugs and are produced in Western Europe and woven from unique synthetic yarn — very plushy and soft.

Made of Carpet has been heavily featured in the media and has a cult celebrity following.

Website:
www.carpet-bags.com

. . .

1. When you were a child what was your dream job and why?

An actress. Sounds silly, I know... It was right until I realized that it is not really a profession, but innate abilities and I do not probably have any.

2. Can you tell me the time that you started to consider yourself successful?

I actually do not remember to feel unsuccessful. I am a person who almost always goes against the current. Initially in the beginning it is always unpleasant and even punishable, but the result is always worth doing as I think is right.

Talking particularly about my fashion brand, the first success came in 2013: our bags were chosen and featured in detective period drama Ripper Street (Season 2, series 3 "Become Man").

I took part in the Lord Mayor parade. We were the first in the 700-year old history of the parade the <u>women only</u> float "Women in the City and Livery". In that year, for the second time in history, the woman became the Lord Mayor – Fiona Woolf. She actually is our customer (I have the photos).

Made of Carpet was privileged to become one of sponsors of the charity event "Newsrooms got talent" — performing, singing and dancing competition of all famous newsreaders from most of the British news channels.

. . .

In 2014 we became a finalist of Drapers Footwear and Accessories Award.

In 2015 we became an official sponsor of BRIT Award men goodie bags.

This year we became Drapers Award finalists again. This time in the Pure-Player category.

3. I'm sure like every business/business person you have faced adversity: how do you motivate yourself and force through the worst times?

Well,... There is one good motto I know: "Do not tell me why 'not,' tell me what did you do to make it 'yes'".

And another: "You do not need to fix 100 people's lives up. Nor 10, nor even 3. You need to fix it up for just one — yourself. Common! Surely you have the strength and intelligence for one."

4. What are the best things about your job?

I am my own boss and I do not need to go to somebody's office and follow somebody's orders.

5. As Tony Robbins says, *"Success leaves clues"*: what are your daily/weekly habits?

My every day's main motto is "What did you do today for tomorrow?".

· · ·

6. What do you think is the most significant barrier to female leadership?

A lot! Family is the most time and resources consuming.

Then most of us do not have a technical brain and we have to spend twice more time to understand how that piece of iron works. Dependence on the opinions of others about our appearance also does not do any good.

7. What women inspire you and why?

Michele Mone.
  She is a real Phoenix risen from the ashes. Knowing where she was born and bred, she had no the slimmest chance to become a brilliant, beautiful and wealthy business woman as she is now.

8. What advice would you give to your 16-year-old self?

Do not spend time and resources for people and activities you do not need.
  Well, when you are 16, it's worth learning normal healthy cynicism.

9. Your instant mindfulness fix...

Party with friends. It gives the possibility to get off the problem and/or thoughts and after some time look at it from another perspective.

. . .

10. And finally something frivolous: best thing about being a woman…

We can turn our weakness to strength, we can use situations and people, when they do not take us seriously, we can let ourselves look and behave silly and we almost always have somebody out there who is willing to pay for champagne.

Top Takeaways from Irina

- "Do not tell me why 'not', tell me what did you do to make it 'yes'"
- What did you do today for tomorrow?
- Don't spend time and resources for people and activities that you do not need
- Turn your weaknesses into strengths
- Have fun with friends.

RACHEL CARRELL

Rachel Carrell is the Founder of **Koru Kids** (The Evening Standard called it "the Airbnb for nannies").

Koru Kids works like this: they match up two local families and one fantastic nanny. Children are looked after together to save time. This allows parents to save 1/3 on the cost of a nanny, plus the nannies get paid 25% more and it's great fun for the kids.

Rachel is originally from the South Coast of New Zealand; she arrived in England in 2002 to study for her Master's degree and never left.

She became CEO of an online doctor's business for 1.3 million patients. She founded **Koru Kids** after having her baby. In 2014 she was named a World Economic Forum "Young Global Leader".

Website:
   www.korukids.co.uk

. . .

1. When you were a child what was your dream job and why?

As a child I read a lot and often lived in a dream world. More than anything, I wanted to be a writer. I still might become one in my retirement (or get really good at patisserie, that's my backup plan).

2. Can you tell me the time that you started to consider yourself successful?

I don't yet. Every time I achieve a goal, I invent a new one. I celebrate stuff for about half a second. I think this is perhaps not ideal! I'm quite a restless soul.

3. I'm sure like every business/business person you have faced adversity: how do you motivate yourself and force through the worst times?

I don't sweat the small stuff—and almost everything is small stuff. It helps a lot to frame things as learning experiences. The best reaction to a disaster is, "How fascinating!" What can we learn from this, what can we do differently in future? If you have this mindset then you can cope with a lot of things.

There are some life events that you can't treat this way, however. Some things are just awful and there's no bright side to be found. I've been very lucky so far in this regard, but I know true tragedy comes to us all eventually.

. . .

4. What are the best things about your job?

It's been such a joy recruiting a team from scratch. I love them. They're so dedicated, so talented, and work so hard because they believe in the mission so much. In previous roles I've never had the opportunity to hand pick every single person for the team, and it's been a massive privilege to do so this time.

It's also really great building a service, which is making families happy every day. We get wonderful feedback about our nannies and our nanny shares. Even if it all fell down tomorrow, we would have done some great work on the way.

Aside from that, I love any parts of the job which are creative and involve building things, whether that's a brand, a website, a process, or a team. I'm a builder by nature.

5. As Tony Robbins says, *"Success leaves clues"*: what are your daily/weekly habits?

I am always carrying a post it notes with my top three priorities on it. I rewrite it frequently and try to be very purposeful with my time and avoid distractions, to make sure I'm always working on the most important things for the business.

Also, I think quite a lot about my own energy and how it changes throughout the day.

Mornings are best for things that require hard thinking or that I don't want to do.

. . .

Evenings are best for tasks which I find fun (like editing a blog post) or which are repetitive things that I don't need to think hard about. I eat a lot of protein to keep my sugar levels stable throughout the day and I know that if I find myself becoming easily distracted, it's probably because I am dehydrated.

6. What do you think is the most significant barrier to female leadership?

I see women voluntarily taking a step back in their career for a period of time while they have small children, but then struggling to get back into the workforce afterwards.

Often they were earning more than their male partners but then the tables turn and while the men power forward, the women's earnings are stagnant. That then means that when someone in the family needs to flex to cope with the everyday needs of the family, it "just makes sense" that it's the woman.

So gradually, bit-by-bit, the woman loses her ability to play a leadership role in the workforce. That's fine if she's chosen that path with her eyes open, but often the women I know didn't really choose it.

For me part of the solution to this is to have men take more of a role in early childhood in the first place. Longer paternity leaves would really help. I think this is slowly changing – I have a few male friends who've taken long breaks of six months or more to look after their kids. There's a long way to go, though.

. . .

7. What women inspire you and why?

I have a friend who is the single mum of four kids, the youngest of which has Down Syndrome. She's got a few difficult people and situations in her past but she's one of the most positive, practical, upbeat people I know. Her resilience is incredible.

I remember when she just had her fourth baby and was trying to lose a lot of weight, walking absolutely miles every day and taking salad with her to mummy meetups. Can't have been easy when we were all eating cake! But she has this strength of character and determination, which I find incredibly inspiring. She's also highly principled, incredibly hard-working and generous.

8. What advice would you give to your 16year old self?

Learn to code. Don't give up on computer science. Keep studying linguistics. Buy Apple stock.

9. Your instant mindfulness fix…

Anything that makes you focus on the present moment works for me as an instant mindfulness fix. It can be as simple as noticing that there's a breeze on your skin, or that the metal leg of the chair is cold on your leg. Focusing for a second on how your body is experiencing the world releases a tiny burst of joy.

10. And finally something frivolous: best thing about being a woman…

I'm pregnant right now and the feeling of my baby kicking me is the most beautiful thing in the world, my little butterfly secret. Although there are lots of difficult bits of being pregnant, there are some utterly wonderful parts as well.

Top Takeaways from Rachel

- Don't sweat the small stuff — frame mistakes as learning experiences
- Carry a post-it note with your top three priorities for the day — keep focused and avoid distractions
- Fit your activities around your own productivity map
- Focus on the present — enjoy
- Look after yourself.

CLAIRE CURZON

C laire Curzon is the Managing Director of **Brighter Directions**, a multi-award winning marketing agency, with clients ranging from innovative SMEs through to global corporations.

Brighter Directions specializes in:

marketing plans & product launch campaigns, PR& comms (press, trade and broadcast globally), social media management, outreach & engagement and direct campaigns.

Claire is also CEO/Board member of Employability Derbyshire, a charity program to develop the workforce of tomorrow throughout the region.

Website:
   www.brighterdirections.co.uk

. . .

1. When you were a child what was your dream job and why?

Journalist – actually, more specifically I wanted to be a News Presenter on BBC news. I loved how glamorous the job looked, and after completing an exercise in school where I acted as a "journalist" on a project, I loved the fact that they sourced information, researched, evidenced and presented that information back, the whole project had me hooked from the word go. Plus... I saw they always had a cuppa on the desk and I'm an avid tea drinker!

2. Can you tell me the time that you started to consider yourself successful?

Wow, this is actually a tricky one. I guess success is measured differently by different people, but for me being 100% honest with myself it was probably more so within the last year or so of operating my own agency, which has been going for twelve years!

During my corporate career in media, I was lucky that my hard work was recognized with advancements, and I was always very satisfied with my roles and teams, but ultimately I always wanted more — which I guess you can consider as success. I think looking back now, I always had in my mind I wanted to run my own business, but it wasn't as clear or focused as it is now.

Thinking about when I thought I was most successful, it probably wasn't fully until a few years ago, when I took the time to self-reflect on my experiences and achievements — looked around my office, looked at our client boards and thought "this is it, I have what I've always wanted".

. . .

3. I'm sure like every business/business person you have faced adversity: how do you motivate yourself and force through the worst times?

Definitely dealing with difficult and unethical clients is the hardest for me. I'm a natural people person, I love people and love seeing others happy and fulfilled, so when we have clients (in the past!) that perhaps don't share my mentality, I find it incredibly hard to deal with and turn into "business" mode from the "relationship" mode I hold naturally.

I keep myself motivated by passion – I'm full of it, and so is my amazing team, we all mirror each other's wins and losses, and for that I think that we all team-motivate as a matter of course.

We all genuinely care about what we do, and our clients success, and although of course some days are harder than others (especially in PR, we have what's called "no days" when nothing ever comes to fruition), but they are just hours and days in what is a lifetime cycle so we try and keep positive and bounce off each other with new ideas and concepts we can try, or simply laugh it off — laughter is the best medicine... or vodka sometimes helps too (I am not advocating drinking in the workplace, but after your time is your own)!

Family is also critical to success and motivation, you need that cushion outside of work, as much as you do in it!

4. What are the best things about your job?

Again people. People are what make the world go around, not money or things.

I work with an amazing group of people who I have hand-selected for their work ethic, skill and abilities and, I think I have the absolute best in the world. They are to me anyway.

Every moment in life, good or bad comes down to people — that is one of our sayings in the office, we try and ensure that our life ethic is reflected in our work too and bring some brightness or sunshine to others, clients, partners, colleagues or suppliers as much as we can!

5. As Tony Robbins says, *"Success leaves clues"*: what are your daily/weekly habits?

I was recently referred to as "an incredibly passionate resolution provider" after explaining to someone our methodology — at first I wasn't impressed by the statement, but on reflection found I agreed. We are a marketing agency, that's what we do — but ultimately it's about us not taking no for an answer and constantly coming up with creative ideas and tactics to generate the best results for our clients. Our habit is one of resilience and stubbornness.

I think a huge part of my/our success is our ethic and environment. We don't have huge posh offices with high-tech furniture and toys, we have a comfortable, friendly, bright (orange, obviously!) and open environment where our team thrives together, you'll often hear shouting across our open-plan office of banter, ideas and collaborations between departments. You don't need flashy things to make an office innovative, you need the right people.

Having thought about my daily habits, here are things I do every day without fail... some maybe irrelevant, but feel free to ignore and take what you wish!

. . .

Read the news — find out what's going on in the world (or your industry), what's new, what's changing, what's being forecast, how can you use that information in your work development, or your clients?

Eat. Sometimes I can go the day without eating, because I'm so busy, and a perfectionist so hate leaving uncompleted tasks — but I always eat breakfast, usually I visit my mum and have it with her after dropping the kids off at school club.

Talk/Share.

We have a strict unsaid process in our business when it comes to quoting for new client proposals – I create all new proposals for the company, but as part of that I have a specific order that I follow which is always the same: conduct initial research, speak to the client to fact-find objectives and needs, more research, then the most important part — we hold an internal team meeting (which constitutes of everyone turning around my desk — never in our conference room) where I give them all the brief and ask "what would you all do?" — everyone has the opportunity to contribute, comment and share ideas from the newbie junior to me — everyone has valid opinions and ideas, that's something I learnt a long time ago, that it's not always the top honcho that has the best ideas, sometimes it's the ones you least expect, so give them a voice.

Manage distractions.

I personally have a diary and I could not live without it.

All important tasks are pre-scheduled in there without fail, (this is EVERYTHING I must do) from calls, appointments, workload tasks through to getting my nails done or leaving on time — it accounts for my every move almost in seconds! Everything else goes on a to-do list, which is completed when I have time.

. . .

Switch off. At the end of the day (or sometimes evening) when I leave the office, that's it — unless something dramatic happens and I need to act, I am finished for the day — or week if it's a holiday. My mobile is off and my time is mine to switch off and spend quality time with family and friends.

Always carry paper and a pen. The best ideas come to you when you least expect it, so be prepared for those moments.

6. What do you think is the most significant barrier to female leadership?

Self-belief and perceptions.

I can only speak for my own experience.

I was lucky in my career that although a hugely dominated environment media is, we had plenty of senior females to pave the way for the future, one of my first immediate line-managers was a very strong and talented female and I was a sponge around her, always admiring her positivity, strength and presence around our male-focused boardroom meetings.

She was one of my first role models and later, my advocate in the company success. Yet, there is still a major gap between women doing great work and women at the top, as well as the perceptions in organizations (of all sizes) that think that women need to believe in themselves much more ...

I read recently that women and men are totally different when referencing abilities. In a test project, equal skilled men and women we're quizzed about their ability to progress — they were given a sheet of paper with all their skills listed, and asked to tick the skills they needed to develop more in order for them to be comfortable to go for the next level (promotion).

Women said they needed 100% — to essentially be perfect at the skills needed before they would even think about progressing ...

How many did men say? 35%!

We all know that most women are perfectionists, especially those at the top, but what this "test" said to me is that women need to have more self-belief and faith in their own ability to be amazing, and then have the confidence to put themselves forward for progression or that campaign they'd love!

More so, women need to acknowledge (loudly) when you are great at something .... And "go for it" if you already think you can, you most certainly can, because we are naturally reserved creatures who plan for the worst!

7. What women inspire you and why?

All women. I think that all women are beautiful, talented and inspirational.

I'm very much an advocate of women everywhere and believe we should support and drive each other to build not only each other, but also the next generation and economies to come.

Strong women who are still women are the most inspirational to me, and by that what I mean is those that are successful and commercial, running and managing great businesses, but those that can also be strong in themselves as a women, know their strengths and know that we, as women don't have to compete with men — they have their place too.

Women are here to offer something different to men, the things that they can't do, building on our strengths, not replicating them in mannerisms, design and stature, because we shouldn't need to. Women are different for a reason.

8. What advice would you give to your 16year old self?

Stay stubborn.

When I was younger I was always called stubborn and bossy — it hasn't changed as I've gotten older, but I have become more comfortable and even proud of those aspects of my character.

Stubborn equals my passion and my perfectionist nature that gets things done, and bossiness equals my ability to manage multi disciplinary projects and campaigns, seeing things through to the end and ensure that things are done properly and well — and the fact that I know my worth and the value that I bring to the table.

9. Your instant mindfulness fix…

A chat with the team, friend or family member — or "blowout" as I call it!

Often when stress is high, all you need is some fresh air, or a fresh approach — so I walk away from my desk, take my cuppa outside and calm down. If that fails I have a rant in the office or vent to the team and they are quick to put me straight back into solution mode... give yourself ten-seconds, then move on!

10. And finally something frivolous: best thing about being a woman...

Everything – what isn't there to love?
We are strong in business, strong at home and strong in ourselves.

Top Takeaways from Claire

- Take time to reflect on your experiences and achievement — you have done more than you think
- Stay stubborn and know your value
- Acknowledge out loud what you are great at and "go for it"
- Women don't have to compete with men, they offer something different, build on that
- When things get though, take time out and calm down.

SALLY BUNKHAM

S ally is a social media strategist at the **PANDAS Foundation**, a charity that supports perinatal mental health.

Sally was previously CEO and Founder of Mum's Back a social enterprise completely , utterly and unashamedly all about new mums.

Website:
   www.pandasfoundation.org.uk

1. When you were a child what was your dream job and why?

When I was a little girl I dreamed of being a vet or working with animals. I had pretty much every pet you could imagine at various points in my childhood ranging from stick insects and African snails right through to dogs and ponies (after much whining and pleading to my poor parents).

•　•　•

2. Can you tell me the time that you started to consider yourself successful?

Oh, that's tricky. My opinion of myself varies daily! I remember shortly after I met my husband he persuaded me to seek a pay rise in the job I had at the time. I had been paid the same amount for a few years, and I was thinking it was time for a promotion.

I called a meeting with my boss and said that unfortunately I would need to move on unless I started earning a little more. She got my job re-graded and I gained a significant pay rise. I was around 26 at the time, and I thought, "Oh hang on, maybe I am worth quite a bit!"

More recently, it felt great when I was asked to be a partner by NOTHS. Mum's Back had only been alive a matter of weeks. It felt like a real accreditation of my hard work and effort that an established and high quality site such as NOTHS was keen to have me. It also enforced my belief that my concept was strong.

3. I'm sure like every business/business person you have faced adversity: how do you motivate yourself and force through the worst times?

The social side/aim of the business really drives me. I don't think I'd have as much fire in my belly to succeed if it wasn't for that. Mum's Back, as well as selling hampers, was raising money for the PANDAS Foundation and awareness of perinatal mental health conditions by writing articles, blogs and more recently TV and radio appearances.

I myself suffered from PND and my experience has given me a real passion for helping others that may be going through similar problems.

It's this side that I think of when the going gets tough, and it helps me dust myself off and get back on the horse!

I am also a member of a couple of online women in business support groups. Helen Packham's "The Courageous Leader's Club" and the Talented Ladies Club's "TLC Business Club". I find the support in those groups invaluable. If I'm having a bad day I can post in there and the other women will pick me up and make me realize I'm not alone.

4. What are the best things about your job?

I love the mix of business and social aim. It gives me a great mix of priorities. I also love the flexibility it brings me. I work incredibly hard, but it's up to me when I put the hours in. Having 2 toddlers this is really important to me. I also love the unpredictability of it all. One day I'm packing up hampers to be sent out, the next I'm appearing on live TV (at a few hours notice!). I find it exciting.

5. As Tony Robbins says, *"Success leaves clues"*: what are your daily/weekly habits?

I always try to have a section of the day where I turn off social media notifications, which can be really distracting. I also try to check in with my FB groups to network with other ladies in business, where I've found some fantastic support. And I try to have each afternoon with my kids without looking at my mobile phone, which can be hard! It's really important to get outside every day.

I find my brain goes a bit mushy if I stay in all day. Fresh air helps.

• • •

6. What do you think is the most significant barrier to female leadership?

Sadly I think that women are more likely to have confidence issues than men. We find it harder to big ourselves up and can have a tendency to downplay our achievements. Perhaps we just have more modesty than men! But that can often work to our detriment. We need to realize our own worth more.

7. What women inspire you and why?

In my personal life I have many friends that inspire me. Many are single mums and I have no idea how they do it.

Celebrity wise I adore Kathy Burke. She's hilarious and had a pretty tough upbringing. She is true to her roots and you can tell she genuinely cares about people.

Business wise I adore my mentor, Helen Packham. She suffered from a loss of confidence when she became a mum, which I can totally relate to, but was able to regain it.

Now she helps other women do the same.
     She has a way of nailing how I'm feeling before I even have! She has always encouraged me to be authentic and to hone my core message, which brilliantly mixes my business and beliefs.

Since working with her I am realizing my own worth and she's given me the confidence to make me want to make a dent in the universe.

. . .

8. What advice would you give to your 16year old self?

It would probably be to eat better and exercise more. I wish I'd known back then how therapeutic exercise could be. I also wish I'd known not to crave the attention of boys that didn't deserve it.

9. Your instant mindfulness fix…

A jog listening to some kind of electronic music. I'm a big fan of Orbital and the Chemical Brothers. If I'm having a bad day I get jogging and stick Orbital's "Rez" on. It usually sorts me out.

10. And finally something frivolous: best thing about being a woman…

Well, I'm not sure it's exclusive to being a woman, but I do love a good night out with my girlfriends, preferably involving a lot of wine.

Top Takeaways from Sally

- Realize your own worth — don't downplay your achievements
- Be authentic and hone your core message
- Get outside — you'll be surprised how much some fresh air can help!
- Take time for yourself and your family — turn off social media ;-)
- Find your tribe/support group.

YASMIN VORAJEE

Yasmin Vorajee is the creator of **Tiny Time Big Results**.
Yasmin is a Coach/Trainer for business owners and entrepreneurs, helping them turn their skills and expertise into a profitable business in 20 hours a week.

Yasmin is feisty about the things she cares about and loves nothing more than seeing people create a life they love, with the money to enjoy it.

Website:
  www.yasminvorajee.com

1. When you were a child what was your dream job and why?

When I was a child, I had so many ideas about what I wanted to do. I was never fixed on doing one thing!

.   .   .

One thing I vividly recall is my desire to teach. I spent many hours in my bedroom teaching my "invisible" class, using the back of my bedroom door as a blackboard.

Which is ironic because now I spend my working hours sitting in the 3rd bedroom in our home, still teaching but now to an audience across the globe. From Hawaii to South Africa to Australia – all from the comfort of my own home in rural Ireland.

2. Can you tell me the time that you started to consider yourself successful?

For a long time, I considered success to be measured according to the number of qualifications I had gained, the amount of money I was making or number of people in my database, and as time has gone by, I have come to the realization that none of these things matter in the grand scheme of things.

I have 3 healthy, happy and beautiful children. I have a husband whom I adore. My family is loving and supportive. I have amazing friends and I get to do what I love every day. That for me, is a life well lived.

3. I'm sure like every business/business person you have faced adversity: how do you motivate yourself and force through the worst times?

Focusing on *why* I do what I do is my go-to strategy. Being there for my family is top of the list for me. Using my talents and skills and putting them to use and *being useful* is important to me.

· · ·

Knowing I can combine the two and make a life, not just a living, keeps me going.

And there have been many ups and downs! When I am tired and wonder why I'm doing what I'm doing and *"wouldn't it be easier just to get a job?"*, I know that's not an option for me. I am open to all sorts of ways of bringing money into the home and feeding our children. But for me, it goes beyond that. It's about doing something with your heart and soul. Making a difference. And that keeps me going.

4. What are the best things about your job?

Freedom, working with people I love, flexibility & creativity. I never thought I was a creative person until I realized creativity exists in all of us — it's birthed in each of us in very different ways. I am creative when it comes to how I share my message; how I brand my work and the work I do with my clients.

5. As Tony Robbins says, *"Success leaves clues"*: what are your daily/weekly habits?

Planning my time, spending at least five minutes each day in silence (can be hard to do with three young children!), planning our meals for the week ahead and going for a walk at least once a day.

6. What do you think is the most significant barrier to female leadership?

Our belief in our ability and worth. I have invested a lot of money and time to learn how to be self-employed and how to grow a business around my skills and talents. But my biggest block has been my lack of self-belief.

Even though I was a former Vice President of Leadership Development and a Chartered Member of the CIPD, I was still crippled with a lack of belief in my abilities and the value I bring to the table. And I see this all the time with my clients. Amazing, brilliant women yet still they are questioning themselves "who am I to do this?".

And the question has to be "who am I not to do this?"!

Strategy will only take you so far. Mindset will take you all the way.

7. What women inspire you and why?

Women who follow their heart and inspire others. Not kick the ladder away once they have climbed it. We are all in this together and your success does not take away from my success.

I am inspired by women who seek to collaborate, not compete. And this isn't "New Age" nonsense. This is about believing in an abundant universe, knowing there is enough for everyone and holding a firm belief that a rising tide lifts all boats.

8. What advice would you give to your 16year old self?

Stop worrying so much about how it will pan out! It doesn't matter if you don't know what you want to do with your life. Simply focus on what you want to do next.

. . .

9. Your instant mindfulness fix...

Close your eyes and take a deep breath! Works a treat every time!

10. And finally something frivolous: best thing about being a woman...

For me, it has to be growing my babies. I loved being pregnant and seeing my three children now, I'm amazed at the miracle my body is and the three miracles it has created!

Top Takeaways from Yasmin

- Find your own definition of success
- Focus on why you do what you do
- Believe in your ability and worth
- Mindset will take you all the way
- Don't kick the ladder away once you climbed it — your success does not take away from others - A rising tide lifts all boats.

UTE AMANN-SEIDEL

U te Amann-Seidel is the Director/Owner of two businesses, creating inspiring transformative experiences in Scotland for people who are curious and want to enjoy and connect with stunning locations at a deeper level:

- **Wild Art** offers art holidays, creative retreats and tailor-made art experiences.
- **Fire & Rain** organizes self-care retreats for widows and widowers.

Ute uses the vast array of skills gathered in her career as Management Consultant - monitoring and evaluations, social impact (SROI - social return on investment), project development, sourcing and applying for funding — to better help her customers.

Websites:
www.wildatartscotland.com
www.fireandrain.scot

· · ·

1. When you were a child what was your dream job and why?

Haha … it was a job I wouldn't fancy now — air hostess! It was at a time when air travel still had something glamorous about it and I loved the idea of traveling around the world for my job. I still love traveling to different countries — but in a more relaxing manner!

2. Can you tell me the time that you started to consider yourself successful?

Working life in general:

- managing projects as a senior consultant in a management consultancy….happy clients and positive feedback from directors told me I must have been doing something right

In my current business:

- when major bereavement support organizations and networks confirmed to me that Fire & Rain offers an important and much needed service.

3. I'm sure like every business/business person you have faced adversity: how do you motivate yourself and force through the worst times?

It's not always easy, but especially since the sudden death of my fiancé I've been taking a very mindful approach to living and working. When things don't go well I kind of observe and question the situation and let my intuition guide me through it.

4. What are the best things about your job?

- Being able to use all that I've learned and experienced to help others — that makes it meaningful.
- The Flexibility of being my own boss.
- Being able to use my creativity in every aspect of my business.

5. As Tony Robbins says, *"Success leaves clues"*: what are your daily/weekly habits?

I start every day with yoga practice — even if it's just five minutes when time is tight. A walk in the beautiful Scottish countryside most days.

6. What do you think is the most significant barrier to female leadership?

Wanting to please others and making ourselves smaller than we are.

7. What women inspire you and why?

Meryl Streep because I admire her talent and authenticity.

My sister-in-love Susan (David and I weren't married yet when he died so we call each other sisters-in-love) for her loving and kind approach to life.

· · ·

8. What advice would you give to your 16year old self?

Make "indestructible self-belief" your mantra and care less what others think.

9. Your instant mindfulness fix...

A walk on my own.

10. And finally something frivolous: best thing about being a woman...

We can wear skirts when it's hot!

Top Takeaways from Ute

- Take a mindful approach to living and working
- Let your intuition guide you
- Make "indestructible self-belief" your mantra
- Care less what others think
- Use what you have learned to help others.

ANNE-SOPHIE WHITEHEAD

Anne-Sophie Whitehead founded **League Network** based on her 15 years leadership at NJ's 5 sport Mountain Top League.

She has been CMO, co-Founder and Director of B2B media and service firms, including Winning Media, Triathlete Magazine, Outsourcing Today, EmployeeService.com , SharedXpertise Media, Corporate Responsibility Media and the American Distilling Institute.

Anne-Sophie holds a MBA in marketing from the Catholic University of Louvain (Belgium), BA in International Business Management from Institute Commercial Nancy (France) and in English from the University of Nancy II (France).

Website:
   www.leaguenetwork.com

1. When you were a child what was your dream job and why?

As a child, I wanted to be a doctor but was worried about not having the math and science skills needed. And during our summer vacation, while working on our family countryside house, I pictured myself refurbishing and flipping houses — even before it was trendy.

Marketing and Business became a focus in High School and I first specialized in international business management and inter-cultural negotiations. In all, I think what motivated me was working any job that required interacting with people and helping them find something they needed (health, house, product and services).

2. Can you tell me the time that you started to consider yourself successful?

I still don't consider myself successful in the business sense of it. Part of being an entrepreneur is to never be satisfied with the status quo. Any professional success means a step toward a new level of challenge.

I measure my success not in money or status but in my personal impact. My kids are great because I became confident in my ability to love who I am. My colleagues are happier because they know I have their back. My customers are succeeding because of what I deliver. To me, this is success. Being proud of what you bring to others. One person at a time.

It doesn't matter if you're outwardly successful if the person inside isn't feeling whole.

. . .

3. I'm sure like every business/business person you have faced adversity: how do you motivate yourself and force through the worst times?

"There are no problems, just solutions". That overused nugget constantly rings through my mind. I was raised to be analytical (and critical). This can slow me down, but it is also a great strength. Faced with a problem, my mind goes into solution mode and cycles through possible outcomes — worst first, then best, then every single possible option in between. There is always a solution in there somewhere.

My other strength is a learned ability to organize crisis into a sequence of events: crisis, assessment (is everyone ok, what's the damage, are we now stable?), options (worst case, best case, what else?), goal setting, then action. Inaction is the worst that can happen to me. So, in a sense, a crisis is always a way to thrust myself into action. It's not always immediate or without tears, but I know that action will ensue, and then I'll be ok.

4. What are the best things about your job?

I have been lucky to be able to afford great flexibility with my schedule.

As a young, single woman that meant picking up and traveling for work 2-3 weeks a month. As a mom, with small kids, I had the luxury to leave work to take my kids to their activities, and work from there, often in my car.

Sometimes it meant getting up at 4.00 am to get a few hours of work before they were up, but I did not have to ask for permission. This is something I wish every woman could have.

· · ·

Now that my kids are older, travel has resumed and I get to share more of my learning with them. I'm also able to say yes to things that excite me without compromising my job. Often it leads to making more connections, business and personal. I am never bored.

And since the launch of League Network last year, I have the greatest time using my professional skills in business to have a positive effect on kids and youth sports, which is what my volunteering activities have revolved around for over a decade. I truly have the best of both worlds.

5. As Tony Robbins says, *"Success leaves clues"*: what are your daily/weekly habits?

Not as good as they should be. Between my two job interests (Founder and COO of League Network, and Deputy Director at the American Distilling Institute), volunteering and family, my schedule is a bit of a mess.

I do have habits that I try not to deviate from:

- I do live by my to-do list and my calendar. Thanks to Google, they sync to make sure I don't miss anything. If a task does not reside on one of them, it doesn't exist
- My mornings always start with reading inspirational and business blogs to spur new ideas
- I avoid personal social media during the day (and only check in a couple times a week either at lunch, or at night)
- I learned to say no and to realize that you can't do everything. Knowing what to let go of is a strength.

6. What do you think is the most significant barrier to female leadership?

Basic gender stereotypes pigeonhole women into roles that they find hard to break out of. Our leadership needs to start in school and at home, where we can break the assumed gender predisposition (macho boys vs obedient girls).

As a personal anecdote, one of my grandfathers, who loved all of his grandchildren unconditionally, would still stay out loud, as we grew into adolescence, that my sister, cousin and I needn't go to college.

He had no problem with my grandmother, or his daughters-in-law being very highly educated. He had no problem with us talking about the careers we wanted, or wielding a hammer. He just wasn't sure it was necessary for us to pursue a degree. He was unaware of the absurdity of the dichotomy, and unable to make a connection between the stereotype he expressed, and the potential damaging message he conveyed to his grand-daughters (never mind his grand-sons).

While they did not shy from opposing his point of view, my aunt and mom did not seek to fight him, but focused on making sure their children would not take the appalling advice to heart. It is our duty, as women, to ingrain inclusivity and fairness in our children (in my mind this goes for all stereotypes) and to surround ourselves with men who support those values.

We need to teach our daughters to never doubt their strengths, and our sons that being a real man means being a true partner. Affirmation of both means that we have a chance to normalize gender relations at a fair level. It starts early, and it needs to be reinforced constantly. At school, in sport, and in business, this means, for now, a conscious effort to combat established bias every step of the way.

7. What women inspire you and why?

This will sound cliché, but my grandmother and mother for the strength they gave me.

Neither one of them would take credit for it, but I would not have had the courage to leave my country at 25 and to decide to marry a man I had met 12 days earlier, without knowing that they loved me unconditionally (as does my dad), and that I had a safe place to come back to anytime.

No questions asked, no judgment passed. I stand on their shoulders, and I make it my business to pass this blessing along to my daughter, and the women I have the chance to help. Strength is the best thing we can bequest to each other.

8. What advice would you give to your 16year old self?

Don't be so hard on yourself, and don't let other people's perceptions put obstacles in your steps. I only learned not to care with age and maturity. People only have the power to hurt you if you let them.

9. Your instant mindfulness fix…

Drop everything, take deep breaths and assess. Do one thing that you can cross off the list. Then another one, until the machine has started again on a steady rhythm.

. . .

My ultimate mindfulness guru should be "The Little Engine That Could" — when everything gets nuts, my mantra becomes "I think I can – I think I can – I think I can – I think I can – I know I can – I know I can…".

10. And finally something frivolous: best thing about being a woman…

Not being a man. I don't envy them.

Top Takeaways from Anne-Sophie

- The ultimate mantra: I think I can – I think I can, I think I can
- There are no problems, just solutions
- Don't be so hard on yourself and don't let other people put obstacles in your steps
- Read inspirational and business blogs to spur new idea
- It doesn't matter if you're outwardly successful if the person inside isn't feeling whole.

JACQUI BURGE

J acqui Burge is the Founder and CEO at **Desk Yogi**.

Jacqui started practicing and teaching fitness, nutrition and yoga in 1994. This passion grew into a dedicated focus on the effects of workplace conditions on an employee's overall wellbeing, aware that the workplace continued, despite all efforts, to be plagued with absenteeism , depression, illness injury and disengagement.

Jacqui launched **Desk Yogi**, providing a comprehensive wellness platform built around state-of-the-art instructional videos on topics including yoga, fitness, mindfulness, meditation and stress reduction, healthy eating, workplace economics, and productivity to all employees in the workplace, at their pace, no matter their fitness level.

Website:
    www.desk-yogi.com

. . .

1. When you were a child what was your dream job and why?

Odd as it may sound my dream job was to be a competitive Ice Skater. I did train daily and worked to compete in the Olympics one day – I never saw myself doing anything else. I found such joy and freedom while skating. It fed me creatively and fired up my competitive spirit.

2. Can you tell me the time that you started to consider yourself successful?

I am still working on this one! When my daughter starred as Jasmine in the musical Aladdin a few weeks ago I considered myself successful. I signified that I had raised her to 14 years old financially and emotionally and I showed up for her. As a result I showed up for me. All of my hard work culminating in her success. In a very non–codependent way!

3. I'm sure like every business/business person you have faced adversity: how do you motivate yourself and force through the worst times?

I learned from a mentor early on — a woman who owned her own businesses and started from the ground up with less than $200 dollars in the bank — that no matter what, show up everyday. Tired – show up. Sad – show up. Happy – show up. Distracted – show up. How ever you show up — show up!

4. What are the best things about your job?

As cheesy as it sounds — meeting new people. The one on one connection and sharing of ideas, teaching what you have learned and having someone mirror that back to you. It is a beautiful thing. I also don't mind going home early on Fridays!

5. As Tony Robbins says, *"Success leaves clues"*: what are your daily/weekly habits?

Each day I wake up an hour earlier than everyone in my home — even the dogs and cats. I have a morning routine that includes a strong cup of coffee, yoga, meditation, prayer and cleaning. It takes about an hour in all, but by the time the kids are awake, I am fully present and available for Mom time. We get ready and eat breakfast together and then we head out for the day.

We come back together at night and usually eat again and just simply hang out. This is the routine that works for my life. 15 minutes of meditation, 15 minutes of yoga, 30 minutes of daydreaming, alone time and cleaning the house so I don't have it all piled up on Saturday.

This is how I recharge and show up for the good things in life.

6. What do you think is the most significant barrier to female leadership?

Men. Just kidding.

This is a hard question. I have been in many situations where I was the only woman on a team and the boss — when I worked in construction. Not sure if it is the most significant but one BIG barrier is having the people who work for you believe you didn't get the job by mistake (relative, relationship, friend). That you truly are qualified.

. . .

7. What women inspire you and why?

This might be an odd one! But Helen Keller is my all time favorite inspiring woman. The courage and determination to communicate with no communication tools and again showing up for the life she has been given without apology.

I am also a big fan of Jackie O – she faced national grief with dignity and class. Again – the theme of showing up I can't seem to get away from it!

8. What advice would you give to your 16year old self?

Don't get married before the age of 21!
   Be kind to others and yourself.
   Sit in silence every day for 15 minutes and listen to you.

9. Your instant mindfulness fix...

Grounding in the space you find yourself in. It takes two minutes.

Feel your feet on the ground. Close your eyes. Notice sound as it enters your ears. Then notice your breathing. Feel the rib cage expand. Notice the air as it leaves your nostrils. One more breath. Let your collar bone slightly rise and allow your shoulders to fall back and down. Pause. Slowly open your eyes. Notice your feet on the ground. Smile. Done.
   That is it. Complete transformation.

. . .

10. And finally something frivolous: best thing about being a woman...

Birthing humans. Birthing an idea. Birthing the authentic self.

Top Takeaways from Jacqui

- No matter what, show up! However you show up, show up!
- Have a morning routine that works for you
- Recharge and show up for life
- Be kind to other others and to you
- Ground in the space you find yourself in.

ANNA COUSINS

Anna Cousins is the Owner/Director of **MyFitZone** - a hub for real people, living real lives that want to be healthy and fit, ensuring the they have everything they need to be motivated, encouraged and empowered on their quest to become healthier and fitter.

MyFitZone provides online personal training helping people become fitter, healthier, stronger and body confident and in the set shape of their life with minimal equipment and smart training.

Website:
   www.myfitzone.co.uk

1. When you were a child what was your dream job and why?

I was obsessed with horses and wanted to work with them, anything outdoors and active was something that I always wanted to do, I was always the child that loved PE and wanted to do everything at sports day and dreamed of being a professional horse rider or jockey.

2. Can you tell me the time that you started to consider yourself successful?

I have not always been in the fitness industry, I built my career from starting as a painter and decorator to operations management to business development and sales in which I had a very successful career.

Over the last three years I have gone through a divorce, moved house five times, lost two jobs, been through times of depression and anxiety, all whilst trying to realize my dreams in the fitness industry.

I spent two years training as a personal trainer and setting up MyFitZone whilst working full time. I decided to take this route as I felt it was my destiny, my purpose in life. I put myself under enormous pressure, it hasn't been an easy ride and it still isn't, but I have pushed through the stressful times and the times where I wanted to give up.

It wasn't until December 2016 that I quit my job and through myself full time into MyFitZone and I realized my success changed at this point, I finally had personal success through my own happiness of doing a job that I was so passionate about and although not at the stage of currently being as financially rewarding as my previous roles, but it has brought me success in the way of contentment, destiny and what I was meant to do — helping others achieve things they never thought possible.

3. I'm sure like every business/business person you have faced adversity: how do you motivate yourself and force through the worst times?

. . .

You will get what you expect. Expect something great to happen for you every day and it will. This is what I say aloud each morning to myself in the mirror, "I expect something good to happen for me today!".

For me, mindset is everything, I have to keep it real and I don't set goals that are unachievable or this results in frustration yourself and you start to feel depressed when you don't achieve it. We all make mistakes; the key is to learn from them and keep on moving.

It is always helpful to have the support and encouragement of those around you to help encourage you when your motivation begins to wane. It may not even be those close to you that give you the most support but this is massively important to me and this is what got me through the worst times.

I have to step back and take time for myself, even if this is just a day off to re-evaluate, I always come back stronger and more motivated to get things done.

The more control that you perceive I have in my life, the more satisfaction and less stress I experience. It also gives me more mental energy because there is less worrying that I might forget something, or procrastinating on something important. I can rest assured, knowing that the important task has already been prioritized.

You also know what day and time you will be addressing it. No longer are there the nagging thoughts reminding you of what you need to do, or to not forget something. This often drains our mental energy and contributes to increased stress, and often in my industry this leads to many people saying to themselves

. . .

"There are much more important things to worry and think about than being healthy, I can worry about that later". Organize yourself and make time for your health, make time for your training, and most importantly make time for yourself, you have to take yourself.

4. What are the best things about your job?

Helping people lead a fitter and healthier life and improve their well being and the results that come from it makes me proud every day. Although my online business is the core of what I do, I absolutely love the satisfaction I get from local classes, festivals and personal training. Witnessing people change their lives for the better, overcoming pain and injury they never thought they would because of what I have shown them is the most rewarding and best thing about my job.

5. As Tony Robbins says, *"Success leaves clues"*: what are your daily/weekly habits?

Fitness and healthy living is my daily habit! My weekly habits are continually improving through coaching and mentoring and providing new information for my followers.

6. What do you think is the most significant barrier to female leadership?

History of male leaders makes it difficult for women to overcome that perception.

. . .

Flexibility in the workplace also makes it difficult for women as the perception that women will just go off and have children and be on maternity leave then come back to work and have the pressure of trying to run a family as well as hold down a successful job.

7. What women inspire you and why?

Dame Kelly Holmes is a massive inspiration to me which is why I am working with her at the Refresh Festival which she is hosting. An exceptional athlete and what she is doing through her charity and motivational talks is something that inspires me everyday.

Karen Brady – not only hugely successful but is inspiring in her role of vice-chairperson of West Ham United Football Club and a life peer in the House of Lords as well as many other prominent positions. The role in a male dominated sport while juggling a family and other positions.

8. What advice would you give to your 16year old self?

I feel that if I hadn't gone through the experiences, heart ache, bad times and good times then I wouldn't be where I am today. My only advice would have been to follow my dreams and passion earlier than I decided to do. To realize those dreams and to not be afraid of going after then.

9. Your instant mindfulness fix

I escape the screen, the cameras, the work and go for a walk to clear my head, this relaxes my mind and gets me into a better state to face any issues. Even if this is just a quick five minute walk — it really helps me unwind.

. . .

10. And finally something frivolous: best thing about being a woman...

The amazing ability to multitask, be able to articulate what we want, to have organizational skills and be able to communicate.

Women are and can be the most empowering and influential people — we just have to accept and love who we are.

I don't see it that women are the inferior sex, in fact we are the superior and doors open to us everyday. It's just how we decide to react to them and it is our mindset and confidence that stop us from truly reaching our goals.

Top Takeaways from Anna

- Find your purpose and what you are meant to do and you will achieve personal success
- Expect something great to happen everyday and it will
- We all make mistakes — the key is to learn
- Follow your dreams and realize them
- Go for a walk to clear your head — relaxes the mind and you are in a better state to face life
- Love who you are as a woman.

PART II

90 DAYS TO YOUR NEW CAREER

THINK THE PART

30 DAYS TO REBOOT YOUR MINDSET

SELF-IMAGE: THE ULTIMATE GLASS CEILING

Think outside the box? What box? The one we keep ourselves in.

There is a box, and it doesn't just affect our way of thinking. It affects our life, our achievements (or failures), our relationships and so on.

Our world and everything in it (career, body, relationships) reflect our mental attitude. There is always something that stops us from achieving our full potential and reaching new heights. Forget about the corporate glass ceiling; we have our own.

Our Self-image. Self-image is our portable box.

What I am talking about here is the subconscious image. The opinion we have of ourselves, our blueprint, forms the roadmap of where we are going (or not) in life. Self-image is the product of past experiences, failures and successes, humiliations. It's the sum of how we have been spoken to, especially in our formative years, by our parents and teachers. The phrases we heard over and over and over until they became ingrained. And they become the box that "boxes" us in.

We can never outperform our Self-image. It holds us hostage to our current results. And that s***s.

As you are now reading this book, I assume you are not happy with your career or are doing ok but can't understand why you keep holding yourself back.

So, let me explain. Self-image is not self-esteem or confidence. It goes deeper.

Self-confidence is the belief in our abilities and talents and is externally focused, e.g. what you can do.

Self-esteem is the core belief about who you are as a person and, typically, how you view yourself (at your best). Both Self-esteem and Self-confidence are critical to wellbeing and mental & physical health.

Self-appreciation (and Self-love) is all about valuing yourself even at your worst and lowest. And accepting who you are right here and right now – with no judgement. But this is a conscious activity, e.g., how you consciously view/understand yourself. So what I am talking about here is the subconscious image.

Self-appreciation and Sef-love are dependent on our Self-image, the built-in regulator.

You see, we all have two images: the one that reflects from the mirror and the one WE see in the mirror.

. . .

This, in turn, is determined by the paradigms that run our life (and mind).

We are all born without any preconception of a woman's place in the world. Or what women can or cannot achieve. Or what constitutes beauty, for that matter. We are born without preconceived notions that we need to "deserve" love. Then, slowly but surely, the mental conditioning from our environment, family, and education kicks in and, unfortunately, stacks up.

And this forms our subconscious Self-image.

SELF-IMAGE THE BUILT-IN REGULATOR

Self-Image is the ultimate internal regulator: every time it looks like we are about to break free, it will bring us back to base like a thermostat.

And, unless we review and update our image of ourselves, all the work to press in our career and life will reach the "temperature" we are comfortable in. Self-sabotage then comes in. And there we start again.

Your world and everything in it reflects your mental attitude toward yourself — your Self-image.

Look around at every aspect of your life – THAT's your ceiling.

Day by day, for the 90 days, we will dig deep to understand what you really want why you want it and work through your limiting beliefs to recreate a self-image that serves you to achieve your career (and life) goals.

#SmashYourCeiling never sounded more appropriate …

DAY 1: THERE IS NOTHING TO FEAR BUT FEAR ITSELF

The Monkey Mind/dump the c*** exercise

Prompt:
What comes to mind when thinking of the word fear?

....

....

....

....

....

....

....

....

....

....

....

....

....

....

....

The fear process

The fear process is one of the most powerful I have ever encountered; I discovered it when reading "Write For Your Life - The Home Seminar For Writers" by Lawrence Block.

I did it then, and I have re-done it each time I start a new project/venture (including this book), both in my professional and personal life.

Fear contributes to our self-sabotage; it keeps us from extending ourselves and taking chances. So we need to bring it (or them) to the open and face it.

"Fear is the mind-killer" - Frank Herbert.

Ready?

Ok, ready or not, here it is — trust me, it is necessary to go through this.

The process goes like this:

A fear I have about .... is that ....

1. If you don't think you have fears about rebooting your career, going for the BIG job, well, you are lying to yourself, hint hint ... For argument's sake, let's pretend you don't have any, or you run out of them, make something up - even if you think they are totally fabricated (the subconscious mind has a way to tell you things ...).

2. Do not judge. If something comes up, don't try to deduce what it means and if it applies to you. Write it down anyway.

3. If a thought arises that is so upsetting that you feel uncomfortable writing it down, write it down anyway!

4. Don't edit your thoughts. And don't waste any time trying to justify what you are writing, telling yourself it is not important and that's not how you really feel. Do not get entangled with thinking that writing your fears down will make them real either. The purpose of this process is to let go of your fears, and you can do so by discharging them from your mind onto the page.

Write as fast as possible, following the process. Do not stop before you've written down a full page as a minimum.

Before you start, think about what brought you here, your professional situation and what you are trying to achieve.

BREATHE.

Breathe again.

Turn the page and start the process.

Go ahead.

A fear I have about rebooting my career is that

....
....
....
....
....
....
....
....
....
....
....
....
....
....
....
....
....
....
....
....
....
....
....
....
....
....
....
....
....
....
....
....

Take a moment to write down some things that fear has kept you from doing throughout your career — things that you really wanted to do.

....

....

....

....

....

....

....

....

....

....

....

....

....

....

....

....

....

....

....

....

....

....

....

....

....

....

....

....

Done?

And now, to move on from here write the following:

"I am now willing to act in the presence of fear. I hereby resolve for the next 90 days to commit to this journey and that I will not allow fear to keep me from doing something I genuinely desire to do".

Then sign your name and date it.

Name ....

Date ....

Enough for today — good job!

3 things to be thankful for

Think back at the topic covered today — what are the 3 things you are grateful for, despite everything? Remember, if you can't think of any — you are not looking hard enough. Think again.

....

....

....

....

....

....

....

....

....

....

....

....

....

....

....

....

....

....

....

....

....

....

....

....

....

....

....

You see? It wasn't that difficult, was it? Great work.

DAY 2: WHERE ARE YOU NOW?

The Monkey Mind/dump the c*** exercise

P**rompt:**
    What comes to mind when thinking of diversity?

....
....
....
....
....
....
....
....
....
....
....
....
....
....

The Overview

We cannot deny that boardroom diversity is increasing although women remain underrepresented. Looking at recent research from Credit Suisse more than 3,000 global companies found that women held 14.7% of board seats in 2015, up by 54% from 2010 (The CS Gender 3000: The Reward for Change, - 2016).

In the Morgan Stanley Capital International (MSCI) study, Women on Boards: Global Trends in Gender Diversity on Corporate Boards, November 2015, out of the 4,218 companies covered women held 15% of board seats up from 12.4% the previous year (73.5% had at least one woman director and 20.1% had boards with at least three women) while in the Deloitte's analysis of nearly 6,000 companies in 49 countries (Women in the Boardroom: A Global Perspective) women held 12% of board seats, of which only 4% at board chair position.

Research from many worldwide organizations have found that three women or more are needed to create a "critical mass," which can lead to better financial performance yet only 20.1% have at least three women.

MSCI found that having three or more women changes the boardroom dynamics and "enhances the likelihood that women's voices and ideas are heard", also resulting in better financial results than those companies who had fewer like 16% higher Return on Sales (ROS), 26% higher Return on Invested Capital (ROIC) and higher Return on Equity (ROE) than companies without (10.1% vs. 7.4%), as well as a superior price-to-book ratio (1.76 vs. 1.56).

They also found incidentally that companies with fewer women on boards had more governance-related controversies than average.

The highest percentages of women on boards can be found in the old continent with Norway (46.7%), France (34.0%), and Sweden (33.6%)

leading the way and the lowest in Taiwan (4.5%), South Korea (4.1%), and Japan (3.5%) — source Credit Suisse.

Countries with specific targets, quotas, and penalties for not meeting regulations have nearly doubled the average percentage of women on boards including the aforementioned Norway, Iceland, Finland, and Sweden (+ 34%) compared to countries without those measures (+18%).

Action Point

It is time to do some research and raise your awareness on this subject, starting from looking at the sector where you are currently working in, or the one that you'd like to be working in and progress, either or both.

Where are your customers based? Market/s?

....
....
....
....
....
....

What are the demographics of these countries?

....
....
....
....
....
....

Who exactly are your customers?

....
....
....
....
....
....
....

What percentage of your company/sector's customer base is female and what is the age range?

....
....
....
....
....
....

Now, look at the company you are working for or with, if you have your business: what is the employee ratio of males to females?

....
....
....
....
....
....

What is the percentage of women in middle management and in leadership positions?

....
....
....
....
....
....

How does it compare to the percentage of men in middle management and in leadership positions?

....
....
....
....
....
....

How does this relate to your sector/company customer base ratio of male to females (I hope you see where I am going here...)?

....
....
....
....
....
....

Is your company male to female ratio at different levels or reflective of your market/s and customer base?

....
....
....
....
....

In February 2017 UN Women, a division of the United Nations dedicated to gender equality and the empowerment of women, unveiled The "Roadmap for Substantive Equality: 2030," in line with and supportive of the concerted global efforts to achieve the 2030 Agenda for Sustainable Development.

The purpose of the Roadmap is to repeal and/or amend discriminatory laws against women whilst ensuring that laws are supportive in general of gender equality & women's human rights.

The UN Women Roadmap for Substantive Equality: 2030 focuses not only in achieving legislative reform but equally, and more crucially, that they are put into practice.

The move from theory to practice, from the legislative framework to roll out and enforcement will require global coordination among different types of international and regional organizations, governments and so on.

The current estimate is that around 90% of the countries worldwide have at least one or more discriminatory law in their legislative framework with many different examples not exclusive to gender pay gap or women in leadership but also failures to adequately tackle violence against women, sexual harassment in public spaces and participation in politics. Gender-discriminatory laws are often rooted in discriminatory social norms, which remain pervasive and are difficult to change.

Action Point

List current social norms you believe to be discriminatory.

....
....
....
....
....
....
....
....
....
....
....
....
....
....
....
....
....
....
....
....
....
....
....
....
....
....

Great job!

3 things to be thankful for

Think back at the topic covered today — what are the 3 things you are grateful for, despite everything? Remember, if you can't think of any — you are not looking hard enough. Think again.

....
....
....
....
....
....
....
....
....
....
....
....
....
....
....
....
....
....
....
....
....
....
....
....
....
....

DAY 3: ONCE UPON A TIME

The Monkey Mind/dump the c*** exercise

P **rompt:**
     What is a woman's place?

....
....
....
....
....
....
....
....
....
....
....
....
....

A woman's place

What a "woman's place" is or seen to be has varied throughout history from warriors, powerful priestesses, and political leaders to portrayals inferior to men and I think looking briefly, very briefly (I'm not going to bore you with history and a historical portrait — it was not the purpose of the book and less than less this workbook) at the position of women at different points in history it can show us how our society has grown and changed and help us to understand the present, including barriers.

Women have gained and lost power at different times in history; if we look at back at the early times in Christian church, women could hold positions of influence equal to men, (even though the Da Vinci Code is a work of fiction, there are indications that Mary Magdalene was once a significant religious leader — an apocryphal gospel of Mary Magdalene was discovered in the late nineteenth century in Egypt – having a gospel in itself is of significance here).

The fourth and fifth centuries AD, however, saw the degrading of women in the writings of people such as Tertullian, Saint Augustine and Saint Jerome blaming Eve, and consequently by association all women, for the downfall of humanity.

The late 1500s is generally seen as the beginning of Modern History with the Renaissance. Yes, women were painted and portrayed beautifully, but this did not really affect women on a day-to-day basis.

A woman's place was defined as the homemaker with strict expectations: women could not vote and were discouraged in owning a business.

Women of aristocratic families (with properties) were often forced/offered into political marriages where all their property then transferred to their husband.

The biggest gains in equality had to wait until the twentieth century, for example, with the Suffragettes successful campaign for women being granted the right to vote. World War one and two also showed that women could contribute to the economy and could work both inside and outside the home, taking men's places in factories.

The sixties and seventies and the advent of feminism further changed some of society's perceptions and, most importantly changed women's own beliefs.

Action point

Think back at three distinctive times in history — your choice: what was a woman's place in those times?

....
....
....
....
....
....
....
....
....
....
....
....
....
....

What did those beliefs mean for/translate to for women?

....
....
....
....
....

Find at least three heroines in those times that succeeded despite those negative perceptions/barriers:

....
....
....
....
....
....
....
....
....
....

What set them apart?

....
....
....
....
....
....
....
....
....
....
....
....
....
....
....

Shorter day today, good job.

3 things to be thankful for

Think back at the topic covered today — what are the 3 things you are grateful for, despite everything? Remember, if you can't think of any — you are not looking hard enough. Think again.

....
....
....
....
....
....
....
....
....
....
....
....
....
....
....
....
....
....
....
....
....
....
....
....
....
....

DAY 4: WHAT ARE YOUR BARRIERS - PART 1

*The Monkey Mind/dump the c*** exercise*

Prompt:

What comes to mind when you hear the word barrier?

....
....
....
....
....
....
....
....
....
....
....
....
....
....

Cultural, religious & family paradigms

It is difficult to talk about religion without insulting/annoying someone somewhere and without being disputed on the interpretation/miss-interpretation of the scripture/s and this section is not meant in any way to be a pontification of the good/evil in religion/s and or the ultimate guide to mainstream religions's views on women.

This section is to recognize and acknowledge that religion has played/is playing and will continue to play a big part in the way different groups of people perceive themselves and others and their definition of "what good looks like" including women and their role in society and that there is a correlation between the two.

Many religions share the same characterizations and expectations of a traditional female role:

- Raise and teach children,
- Maintain a Godly household,
- Assist the husband decisions,
- Retain and care for family & familial assets.

I'm not saying that religion is the problem but mainly one of the potential restrictions. Sexism, misogyny and patriarchy and attitudes exist often entangled with other social and political factors and ways of thinking, including religion.

When I say patriarchy I mean a system of power relations between men and women, where men and women are complicit and agential, and which privileges particular kinds of gender and sexual identities (usually heterosexual men) over others. These power relations are part of the inner structural personal system with your entire personal image built on this — your belief foundation — which determines what you believe you can and cannot do, how should you do it and why.

Action Point

Now is the time to take stock and look back, not to judge and/or recriminate but to understand and then move on: what effect do you think your own cultural background, religion and family paradigms had including your own reaction to those and how have they limited you-if they did that is (I know these are sensitive subjects, nevertheless, like an addict, it is time to face reality).

Be honest (yes, you need to do some work here :-)).

....
....
....
....
....
....
....
....
....
....
....
....
....
....
....
....
....
....
....
....
....
....
....

For women who wish to have children, there are also the obviously added barriers of going through the gestation period, the birth and consequent time needed to care for a newborn and beyond.

There is the physical barrier (not everyone has an easy pregnancy and is able to continue to perform to the same level/with the same intensity — the time-off pre/post — part) together with the childcare requirements.

Society is made of tribal congregations (religious and secular institutions, communities and families) all with their individual, sometimes divergent and sometimes mutually supportive views of a "woman's place," a "mother's duty" and "the right way of doing things".

Action Point
What are your inherited views about motherhood and a "mother's duty"?

....
....
....
....
....
....
....
....
....
....
....
....
....
....
....
....
....
....

Are these views supportive or conflicting with your desire for professional success and climbing the ladder? How so?

....
....
....
....
....
....
....
....
....
....
....
....
....
....
....
....
....
....
....
....
....
....
....
....
....
....
....
....

Gosh, that was heavy - You need a break for today.

3 things to be thankful for

Think back at the topic covered today — what are the 3 things you are grateful for, despite everything? Remember, if you can't think of any — you are not looking hard enough. Think again.

....
....
....
....
....
....
....
....
....
....
....
....
....
....
....
....
....
....
....
....
....
....
....
....
....
....

DAY 5: WHAT ARE YOUR BARRIERS - PART 2

The Monkey Mind/dump the c*** exercise

P**rompt:**
   What comes to mind when you hear the words "good girl"?

....
....
....
....
....
....
....
....
....
....
....
....
....
....

The "good girl syndrome"

Although there is definitely the outer game of society/family paradigms and so on, there is also a far more important inner game, your own perceptions, your own decisions, belief systems that drive behavior and choices made — the "good girl syndrome".

Rachida Dati comes to mind, the French Justice Minister under French President Nicolas Sarkozy who went back to work five days after having her first child by Caesarean section. Seeing her going back as what is perceived (by whom?) too soon started a barrage and ping-pong of comments and articles, some quite bitching and derogative and some alleging bullying from Sarkozy (and the worse ones were from women).

Even the way she was described ("impossibly glamorous and thin") had negative connotations (like what-all new mothers must look/are fat and frumpy??).

Better still, people were discussing if she is *"right to put the demands of her career ahead of her child? Or is she crazy to miss out on some of the most precious months of her life? "* like there is only one way of being a mother AND a career woman at the same time.

Action Point

How much have your cultural/religious and family paradigms conditioned your views on what a "good girl" behaves like?

....

....

....

How much has it affected your career aspirations and/or choices?

....
....
....
....
....
....
....
....
....
....
....
....
....
....
....
....
....
....
....
....
....
....
....
....
....

Short day today — great job.

3 things to be thankful for

Think back at the topic covered today — what are the 3 things you are grateful for, despite everything? Remember, if you can't think of any — you are not looking hard enough. Think again.

....

....

....

....

....

....

....

....

....

....

....

....

....

....

....

....

....

....

....

....

....

....

....

....

....

....

DAY 6: WHAT ARE YOUR BARRIERS - PART 3

The Monkey Mind/dump the c*** exercise

Prompt:
   What comes to mind when you hear the words "bias"?

....
....
....
....
....
....
....
....
....
....
....
....
....
....

Who's a "good girl"?

Today we are going to delve deeper and this time into "your" idea of a "good girl".

Action point

Following from yesterday's exercises you should now have a good idea of your beliefs derived from the social/religious and family paradigms regarding the "good girl" syndrome (if you can't remember, go and take a look — go on .... I'll wait ;-)).

Now think back at times when you applied this "learnt judgement" and passed it onto others: go as far back or as near as you need to. Actually, I invite you to do so on purpose and see how and if your behavior changed with time.

Describe three different occasions at three different times in your life when you have demonstrated bias towards other women — or yourself — based on the learnt "good girl" syndrome belief (it is hard to admit, but we all do it and we all project our beliefs with our behavior — the point here is to have awareness).

....
....
....
....
....
....
....
....
....
....
....
....
....

....
....
....
....
....
....
....
....
....
....
....

How would you/could behave differently now, if the same situations arise again?

....
....
....
....
....
....
....
....
....
....
....
....

With understanding and acknowledging your own biases, you are taking step forward to a more level playing field — for yourself and other women. Congratulations.

3 things to be thankful for

Think back at the topic covered today — what are the 3 things you are grateful for, despite everything? Remember, if you can't think of any — you are not looking hard enough. Think again.

....
....
....
....
....
....
....
....
....
....
....
....
....
....
....
....
....
....
....
....
....
....
....
....
....
....

DAY 7: REST, RELAXATION AND SOME REFLECTION

The Monkey Mind/dump the c*** exercise

P **rompt:**
   Self-belief

....
....
....
....
....
....
....
....
....
....
....
....
....
....
....

This page is intentionally left blank

3 things to be thankful for

Think back at the topic covered today — what are the 3 things you are grateful for, despite everything? Remember, if you can't think of any — you are not looking hard enough. Think again.

....

....

....

....

....

....

....

....

....

....

....

....

....

....

....

....

....

....

....

....

....

....

....

....

....

DAY 8: REST, RELAXATION AND SOME REFLECTION

The Monkey Mind/dump the c*** exercise

P **rompt:**
     Time for self

....
....
....
....
....
....
....
....
....
....
....
....
....
....

This page is intentionally left blank

3 things to be thankful for

Think back at the topic covered today — what are the 3 things you are grateful for, despite everything? Remember, if you can't think of any — you are not looking hard enough. Think again.

....
....
....
....
....
....
....
....
....
....
....
....
....
....
....
....
....
....
....
....
....
....
....
....
....
....
....

DAY 9: SUCCESS IS A RELATIVE THING - PART 1

The Monkey Mind/dump the c*** exercise

P**rompt:**
   What comes to mind when you hear the word SUCCESS?

....
....
....
....
....
....
....
....
....
....
....
....
....
....

What does success mean to you?

Success means so many things to so many people; if you don't define what good (or great) looks like, you will be always chasing something, the next shiny object, unachievable targets and never be quite satisfied.

Action Point

Pause for a minute and think — jot down what is your definition of success.

....
....
....
....
....
....
....
....

Where does this definition originate from (family, friends, peers)?

....
....
....
....
....
....
....
....

Is this definition still relevant to you now? If yes (or no), why yes (or no)?

....
....
....
....
....
....
....

Has this definition changed in the last few years? If yes, what has changed?

....
....
....
....
....
....
....

What has been the constant (as compared to the variable) in your definition of success?

....
....
....
....
....
....

Well done.

3 things to be thankful for

Think back at the topic covered today — what are the 3 things you are grateful for, despite everything? Remember, if you can't think of any — you are not looking hard enough. Think again.

....
....
....
....
....
....
....
....
....
....
....
....
....
....
....
....
....
....
....
....
....
....
....
....
....
....
....

DAY 10: SUCCESS IS A RELATIVE THING - PART 2

The Monkey Mind/dump the c*** exercise

P **rompt:**
   What do you feel when you hear the words GLASS CEILING?

....
....
....
....
....
....
....
....
....
....
....
....
....
....

What does success really mean to you?

Success means so many things to so many people; we have looked at what is your definition of success and how that has changed from a rational viewpoint. Now is the time to go deeper into your feelings.

Action point

Take some time to think about what success really means to you: a job well done? Position? Power?

....

....

....

....

....

....

....

How would you know you have arrived?

....

....

....

....

....

....

....

What is the feeling that success/THE job will give you?

....

....

....

....

....

....

What is really important to you:

- *Respect from colleagues / family / friends*
- *Financial security/money?*
- *Fulfilling expectations (family/friends/society)?*
- *Other?*

....
....
....
....
....
....
....

What is the destination and why? What will it give you?

....
....
....
....
....
....
....

What will make you feel truly successful?

....
....
....
....
....
....

How can you start feeling that now? Once you understand what success means to you, you can then recognize it and celebrate it — daily. Feeling successful, fulfilled breathes confidence — the more you recognize your achievements and feel good about them — the more confident you feel and the bigger things you will attempt, get my drift? ;-)

.

....

....

....

....

....

....

....

....

....

....

....

....

....

....

....

....

....

....

....

....

....

....

....

....

Great job.

3 things to be thankful for

Think back at the topic covered today — what are the 3 things you are grateful for, despite everything? Remember, if you can't think of any — you are not looking hard enough. Think again.

....
....
....
....
....
....
....
....
....
....
....
....
....
....
....
....
....
....
....
....
....
....
....
....
....
....

DAY 11: WHAT IS YOUR WHY?

The Monkey Mind/dump the c*** exercise

Prompt:
    What do you need?

....
....
....
....
....
....
....
....
....
....
....
....
....
....

The Maslow Hierarchy of Needs

Maslow Hierarchy of Needs is one of the best-known motivational theories trying to understand what drives
"Humans".

Abraham Maslow, a human psychologist, explained this concept in his 1943 paper "A Theory of Human Motivation" and his subsequent book "Motivation and Personality" stating that our actions are motivated so to satisfy certain needs.

Maslow suggests that people are motivated to fulfill basic needs before moving on to the more advanced needs, trying to understand what makes people happy and the things that they do/would to fulfill their needs.

His belief was that people have an innate need and desire to be all they can be but to do so they must meet first a number of more basic needs (the most common representation of this theory is often a pyramid, moving from most basic needs at the bottom to the most complex at the top).

According to Maslow there are five different levels starting at the lowest known as physiological needs.

The bottom of the pyramid has the most basic physical requirements including the need for food, water, sleep, and warmth, and once these are satisfied and people progress up the pyramid, and then these become more and more psychological and social, and so on, all the way to self-actualization, e.g., growing and developing as a person in order to achieve own potential.

Physiological, security, social, and esteem needs are what we would call deficiency needs, arising from lack and satisfying them is important in order to avoid unpleasant situations.

On the other hand at the highest levels of the pyramid are growth needs, which do not stem from deprivation, but rather from a desire to grow as a person.

The need for security and safety then becomes primary and it is all about control and order in our lives and consequent behaviors (financial security, health and wellness, safety against accidents and injury).

The need for appreciation and respect, e.g., gaining the respect and appreciation of others leads to the need to accomplish things and then have efforts recognized together with the feeling of accomplishment and prestige, self-esteem and personal worth.

Self-actualization - "What a man can be, he must be," is the need people have to achieve their full potential as human beings.

"It may be loosely described as the full use and exploitation of talents, capabilities, potentialities, etc. Such people seem to be fulfilling themselves and to be doing the best that they are capable of doing... They are people who have developed or are developing to the full stature of which they are capable," - Abraham Maslow.

Similarly to Maslow Tony Robbins, in his programs and many books, talks about in a more fluid & less hierarchical way the same drivers of human behaviors:

- Certainty and security
- Uncertainty and variety
- Significance
- Love & Connection
- Growth
- Contribution.

It is important here not to be too rigid about the standard progression of the needs within the pyramid: what is more important or indeed essential to one person might not be to others (except perhaps the basic physiological needs that are vital to our survival and essential to the survival and propagation of the species).

My point here is that, on top of the infrastructural belief system based on cultural, religious (or non-religious) & family paradigms, there are basic human needs that need to be fulfilled.

Action Point

This is a good time for a pause and to reflect: looking either at Maslow's pyramid or Tony Robbins's list which one/s of those need/s is/are the most important to you?

How are you fulfilling them right now?

....
....
....
....
....
....
....
....
....
....
....
....
....

What is your why (for that coveted glass/ceiling position)? Are you trying to satisfy your needs or responding to external expectations?

....

....
....
....
....
....
....
....
....
....
....
....
....
....

Refer back to your definition of success and what THE position/s would give you? Were you really honest (with yourself)?

....
....
....
....
....
....
....
....
....
....
....
....

You are doing great.

3 things to be thankful for

Think back at the topic covered today — what are the 3 things you are grateful for, despite everything? Remember, if you can't think of any — you are not looking hard enough. Think again.

....

....

....

....

....

....

....

....

....

....

....

....

....

....

....

....

....

....

....

....

....

....

....

....

....

DAY 12: WHAT IS THE PRICE?

The Monkey Mind/dump the c*** exercise

P rompt:
   What is your price?

....
....
....
....
....
....
....
....
....
....
....
....
....
....

Everyone pays a price

There is a perception that women (even more so women with children) pay a price to rise to the top of an organization/field , etc., (as opposed to it is easy for men?).

Let's face it:

Leadership requires 100% commitment – Everyone pays a price.

Action Point

This point is really important: if the "price to pay" for success/the position is perceived as "too big/painful" and/or unfair, there will always be an invisible barrier, like a force field stopping you from getting there.

Take some time to think what would be the sacrifices you'd have to make to achieve the top positions/dream job , etc.

Are they real or perceived? And, most importantly, are you willing to make them?

....
....
....
....
....
....
....
....
....
....
....
....
....

....
....
....
....
....
....
....
....
....
....
....

Are you making them too big? Are you self-sabotaging? If yes, what are you scared of? No BS here, we are all scared of something, write down your fears.

OK, done?

STOP IT!

Stop making excuses, It is all B*****t.

In the 2015 Global Entrepreneurship Monitor (GEM) Special Report on Women Entrepreneurship, women's entrepreneurship rose by 6% world-wide in the last two years.

According to the 2016 Kauffman Index of Start-up Activity, in the United States women make up 40% of new entrepreneurs (highest since 1996). In the MasterCard Index of Women Entrepreneurs 2017 (MIWE) women's business ownership across the 54 markets measured make up between 25-35% of total business owners.

On Day 2 – *Where are we now* — we have seen the statistics on women on boardroom representation according to some recent reports (respectively 14,7% Credit Suisse, 15% Morgan Stanley and 12% Deloitte using different samples). The barriers are the same including childcare.

And on that note, I'll leave you to ponder...

3 things to be thankful for

Think back at the topic covered today — what are the 3 things you are grateful for, despite everything? Remember, if you can't think of any — you are not looking hard enough. Think again.

....
....
....
....
....
....
....
....
....
....
....
....
....
....
....
....
....
....
....
....
....
....
....
....
....
....
....

DAY 13: PERFECTION IS BORING - BE AWESOME INSTEAD

The Monkey Mind/dump the c*** exercise

P rompt:
   What comes to mind when thinking of perfection?

....
....
....
....
....
....
....
....
....
....
....
....
....
....

Wonder Woman does not exist

The idea that you should take as little maternity leave as possible, work until your waters break beneath your desk, never complain of sickness, swollen ankles and/or backache, and then go back to work fast and/or go back to work and (as much as you love your baby and being a mum) enjoying being back to work and more than baby-talk, but feeling guilty all the way through it, and then coming back home and be the "perfect" wife/partner/significant other (whatever you like to be called) and cooking, cleaning, tidying and putting the baby to bed is ludicrous.

Silence your inner critic — do you and what works for you.

Action Point

Does the picture described above sound like someone you know? Maybe intimately? What are the things that you do to please your inner critic?

....
....
....
....
....
....
....
....
....
....
....
....
....
....
....
....
....

The practicality of looking after a child, and who is going to do it post return to work exists and unfortunately, no matter the progress made recently, we can't deny that women, in the vast majority of cases, still bear the burden of household and family responsibility. That means women in general and even more so women aspiring to leadership positions have to juggle even more than their male counterparts.

All the employment laws on maternity, paternity, shared parental leave and flexible working mean absolutely nothing unless men take up/opt for these opportunities and support their partner/wife/significant other. It is easy to criticize "society," the government, businesses , etc., and ask for more laws, more rules to aid women coming back to work and pursuing a career/leadership and talk about what "men should do more".

Society is made of families and individuals and the change will happen and can happen — starting from your family and your partner taking up a fair share of childcare/household duties and so on.

Relationships do break up sometime but this does not nullify paternal responsibilities and accountabilities in raising children irrespectively of how much you might dislike/hate/can't stand your ex-partner and their new life (of course there might be fathers/parents who are unfit although let's consider this for argument sake to be an exception than the rule).

Think of your family unit as a business with 2 main shareholders whereby the decisions made are for the best interest of the "business"/family unit whilst not stifling ambitions and/or disadvantage either and/or both shareholders.

Too many times men request flexible working and or parental leave (and/or maternity leave) only and exclusively when their wife/partner/significant other already earns more than they do, far more rarely when they are on equal earning footing or thereabouts .The discussion needs to happen about your mutual ambition and career aspiration together with shared responsibilities and potential support needed (in what forms and by whom).

True feminism means accepting both the reality of motherhood, and celebrating its real value personally and to society as a whole but also having equal opportunities and being able to make a choice on how you would like to deal with your career and motherhood without having to apologize if you are ambitious and want to go back to work as soon as, or take a few years off.

Action Point

This is the time to look inside your own relationship – I don't want to cause breakups, nevertheless you know what needs doing here...

....
....
....
....
....
....
....
....
....
....
....
....
....
....
....
....
....
....

3 things to be thankful for

Think back at the topic covered today — what are the 3 things you are grateful for, despite everything? Remember, if you can't think of any — you are not looking hard enough. Think again.

....

....

....

....

....

....

....

....

....

....

....

....

....

....

....

....

....

....

....

....

....

....

....

....

....

....

DAY 14: REST, RELAXATION AND SOME REFLECTION

The Monkey Mind/dump the c*** exercise

P rompt:
    Forgiveness

....
....
....
....
....
....
....
....
....
....
....
....
....
....
....

This page is intentionally left blank

3 things to be thankful for

Think back at the topic covered today — what are the 3 things you are grateful for, despite everything? Remember, if you can't think of any — you are not looking hard enough. Think again.

....
....
....
....
....
....
....
....
....
....
....
....
....
....
....
....
....
....
....
....
....
....
....
....
....
....

DAY 15: REST, RELAXATION AND SOME REFLECTION

The Monkey Mind/dump the c*** exercise

P**rompt:**
   Self-respect

....
....
....
....
....
....
....
....
....
....
....
....
....
....
....

This page is intentionally left blank

3 things to be thankful for

Think back at the topic covered today — what are the 3 things you are grateful for, despite everything? Remember, if you can't think of any — you are not looking hard enough. Think again.

....

....

....

....

....

....

....

....

....

....

....

....

....

....

....

....

....

....

....

....

....

....

....

....

....

....

DAY 16: THINK OUTSIDE THE BOX: WHAT BOX? THINK THE PART

The Monkey Mind/dump the c*** exercise

P rompt:
  Journey

....
....
....
....
....
....
....
....
....
....
....
....
....
....

The Journey - Part 1

OK, you want to be CEO of a (Global) Company or Director of Paper-clips (whatever takes your fancy); you can map out how you can get there and the first point is a "thinking map-journey".

What do I mean by that?

Each role from junior management to leadership/director/board level has different thinking requirements:

- From the here and now action-oriented operational and problem solving way of thinking,
- To the tactical/fluid and then
- Strategic/long term/future forward way of thinking, anticipating what customers might want/need in 10/20 years time whilst staying original and true to the brand AND beating the competition.

Plus cross-functional and P&L/financial implications thinking.

This is when mapping comes useful.

For the next exercise gather together job descriptions from junior management to the highest functional /board director/VP and CEO (whatever is available within your company — either from currently advertised vacancies or job catalogue). Alternatively you can check on job boards for different vacancies in companies similar to yours/in companies you'd like to work for.

. . .

It is a useful exercise to show the difference in requirements across different jobs.

Action point

Gather at least ten different job descriptions starting from your next level up to board level (I also suggest mixing it up e.g. job descriptions at different levels from different functions, not just the one you are working in — for example if you are in marketing also look at finance, sales, customer service , etc.). Read and understand — what are the verbs used? Which ones are the most common cross functionally?

....
....
....
....
....
....
....
....
....
....
....

What is the difference between the current role to the immediate next role and the ultimate role?

....
....
....
....
....
....
....
....
....

How can you apply a higher level of thinking and expand your mind in your current role?

....
....
....
....
....
....
....
....
....
....
....
....
....
....
....

Depending where you are right now in your career, you can see how many steps along the way, how to maneuver in between whilst keeping an eye on the end game. Write it down.

....
....
....
....
....
....
....
....
....
....
....
....

3 things to be thankful for

Think back at the topic covered today — what are the 3 things you are grateful for, despite everything? Remember, if you can't think of any — you are not looking hard enough. Think again.

....

....

....

....

....

....

....

....

....

....

....

....

....

....

....

....

....

....

....

....

....

....

....

....

....

DAY 17: THINK OUTSIDE THE BOX: WHAT BOX? THINK THE PART

The Monkey Mind/dump the c*** exercise

P rompt:
   Destination

....
....
....
....
....
....
....
....
....
....
....
....
....
....

The Journey - Part 2

Today let's work on identifying the top areas (of thinking) that also appear in your own job description, and in each of the job descriptions you have collated/gathered.

Start with the areas more aligned to your strengths (I follow the Tim Ferriss way of thinking — it is better to focus on your strengths than your weakness — this is because in working on your strengths it will be easier and quicker to maximize the improvements and achieve greatness while working).

Action point

Firstly what are your main strengths and talents (things you do extremely well with minimum effort, easily and enjoy)?

....
....
....
....
....
....
....
....
....
....
....
....
....
....
....
....
....
....
....

What are the top areas (of thinking) that you have identified as common between your current role and your future role?

....
....
....
....
....
....
....
....
....
....
....
....
....
....
....

Now combine the two: your top strengths and talents that support/can support the top areas of thinking identified for your future role/s.

....
....
....
....
....
....
....
....
....
....
....
....
....

Next, what can you start doing right now to work on the strengths that serve you the most (for the purpose of climbing the career ladder)?

....

....

....

....

....

....

....

....

....

....

....

....

....

To close the day I'd like to point out one thing: being at the top of any organization can be lonely.

Many times difficult decision/s need to be made, incredibly unpopular decisions that affect thousands of people (sometimes negatively) but they are for the long term longevity of the organization and its greater good — this includes compromises.

If making these types of decisions makes you uncomfortable, it is time perhaps to rethink if you really want the top job/climb the ladder after all.

Yes, you could be the conscience in the boardroom — nevertheless, sometimes, these decisions must be made and you need to be prepared to do so.

3 things to be thankful for

Think back at the topic covered today — what are the 3 things you are grateful for, despite everything? Remember, if you can't think of any — you are not looking hard enough. Think again.

....
....
....
....
....
....
....
....
....
....
....
....
....
....
....
....
....
....
....
....
....
....
....
....
....
....

DAY 18: THINK OUTSIDE THE BOX: WHAT BOX? THINK THE PART

The Monkey Mind/dump the c*** exercise

P rompt:
Gap

....
....
....
....
....
....
....
....
....
....
....
....
....
....

Welcome You Plc.

Keeping in mind the end destination helps when making career decisions: along the way each role — upward or sideways — should be a stepping-stone to the ultimate goal.

But how do you practice whilst waiting for the next role to come along?

Well, you can start by applying a higher level thinking to the You (family / life , etc.) Company - start looking at your own life / family etc.as a Plc. (remember the two shareholders and parental / household responsibilities?).

Action point

What is your brand/what is important to you?

....

....

....

....

....

....

....

....

....

....

....

....

....

....

....

....

....

Who are your main stakeholders/customers/consumers?

....
....
....
....
....
....
....
....

How can you satisfy their needs whilst staying true to you?

....
....
....
....
....
....
....
....
....
....
....

What's the long term plan?

....
....
....
....
....
....
....
....
....

Identify your assets, liabilities, risks, income streams & financial goals (start a Profit & Loss sheet?) and so on.

....
....
....
....
....
....
....
....
....
....
....
....
....
....
....
....
....
....
....
....
....
....
....
....
....
....
....
....

Your life is like your own business...

3 things to be thankful for

Think back at the topic covered today — what are the 3 things you are grateful for, despite everything? Remember, if you can't think of any — you are not looking hard enough. Think again.

....
....
....
....
....
....
....
....
....
....
....
....
....
....
....
....
....
....
....
....
....
....
....
....
....
....

DAY 19: THINK OUTSIDE THE BOX: WHAT BOX? THINK THE PART

The Monkey Mind/dump the c*** exercise

P rompt:
   Gap

....
....
....
....
....
....
....
....
....
....
....
....
....
....

Build your map

Action Point

Mapping time: looking back at what has just been presented, prepare a map of different ways of thinking required at different levels (I would suggest up to the next three roles).

Area left blank for doodling/designing a map.

Choose the top three: how can you start applying these three different levels of thinking to your current role?

....
....
....
....
....
....
....
....
....
....
....
....
....
....

Write down all the ways that you can start applying and practice these three different levels of thinking outside work.

....
....
....
....
....
....
....
....
....
....
....
....
....

3 things to be thankful for

Think back at the topic covered today — what are the 3 things you are grateful for, despite everything? Remember, if you can't think of any — you are not looking hard enough. Think again.

....
....
....
....
....
....
....
....
....
....
....
....
....
....
....
....
....
....
....
....
....
....
....
....
....
....

DAY 20: THINK OUTSIDE THE BOX: WHAT BOX? THINK THE PART

The Monkey Mind/dump the c*** exercise

P **rompt:**
   Think outside the box

....
....
....
....
....
....
....
....
....
....
....
....
....
....

Review time

Action point

By now you should have a clear view of your own personal barriers, your own definition of success, your what and why, know the price and decided to go for it plus a map of the next three roles. Time to link them up...

....
....
....
....
....
....
....
....
....
....
....
....
....
....
....
....
....
....
....
....
....
....
....
....
....
....
....
....

3 things to be thankful for

Think back at the topic covered today — what are the 3 things you are grateful for, despite everything? Remember, if you can't think of any — you are not looking hard enough. Think again.

....

....

....

....

....

....

....

....

....

....

....

....

....

....

....

....

....

....

....

....

....

....

....

....

....

....

....

DAY 21: REST, RELAXATION AND SOME REFLECTION

The Monkey Mind/dump the c*** exercise

P **rompt:**
   Women and friendships

....
....
....
....
....
....
....
....
....
....
....
....
....
....

This page is intentionally left blank

3 things to be thankful for

Think back at the topic covered today — what are the 3 things you are grateful for, despite everything? Remember, if you can't think of any — you are not looking hard enough. Think again.

....
....
....
....
....
....
....
....
....
....
....
....
....
....
....
....
....
....
....
....
....
....
....
....
....

DAY 22: REST, RELAXATION AND SOME REFLECTION

The Monkey Mind/dump the c*** exercise

P**rompt:**
  Sisterhood

....
....
....
....
....
....
....
....
....
....
....
....
....
....

This page is intentionally left blank

3 things to be thankful for

Think back at the topic covered today — what are the 3 things you are grateful for, despite everything? Remember, if you can't think of any — you are not looking hard enough. Think again.

....
....
....
....
....
....
....
....
....
....
....
....
....
....
....
....
....
....
....
....
....
....
....
....
....

DAY 23: THINK OUTSIDE THE BOX: WHAT BOX? THINK THE PART

The Monkey Mind/dump the c*** exercise

P **rompt:**
   Peer group

....
....
....
....
....
....
....
....
....
....
....
....
....
....

Bridge the Gap - peers

"You are the average of the five people you surround yourself with" – **Napoleon Hill**.

This is true financially, emotionally, standard wise and is applicable here too. Finding and connecting with people who are already there, asking questions on their decision-making process — what, why, how they make decisions, critical paths.

"[Emerging] leaders need mentors to guide them, but they also need a network of peers, to reassure them that they are not on the path alone".
Alyse Nelson – President and CEO, Vital Voices.

Action point
Describe your current professional peer group.

....
....
....
....
....
....
....
....
....
....
....
....
....

"People will perform at the level of expectation of their peers. If you surround yourself with peers who expect you to perform at a higher level you will perform at that level to achieve the level of expectation of those surrounding you," - **Tony Robbins**.

How aligned and supportive of your aspirations/ambitions is your current peer group?

....

....

....

....

....

....

Is your current peer group challenging/pushing you to be the best version of yourself? If not, why not? If yes, how?

....

....

....

....

....

....

Think back at last week's exercises and the next two levels up on your map. Based on those two next level roles — identify a potential new peer group that can and will challenge you.

....

....

....

....

....

....

What are the professional associations in our field/sector that you can join to both up-skill yourself and network? List at list five possible organizations.

....
....
....
....
....
....
....
....
....
....
....
....
....

Now it is time to look for networking opportunities to meet your new peer group and level up your strategic thinking. Look up at least at two events per week for the next three months

....
....
....
....
....
....
....
....
....
....
....
....

That's it for today, good job.

3 things to be thankful for

Think back at the topic covered today — what are the 3 things you are grateful for, despite everything? Remember, if you can't think of any — you are not looking hard enough. Think again.

....
....
....
....
....
....
....
....
....
....
....
....
....
....
....
....
....
....
....
....
....
....
....
....
....
....
....

DAY 24: THINK OUTSIDE THE BOX: WHAT BOX? THINK THE PART

The Monkey Mind/dump the c*** exercise

P **rompt:**
   Mentor

....
....
....
....
....
....
....
....
....
....
....
....
....
....

If you want to be the best, you need to learn from the best – I have not invented this phrase — you can hear it for the lips of the most successful entrepreneurs, CEOs, billionaires out there. And that is the point.

You need someone who has been there, seen it, done it and got the t-shirt so to speak and you can emulate exactly what he or she has done and shortcut your way to success.

This is applicable to both people you associate with on a daily basis and to choosing mentors to speed your journey.

> *"If you want to be successful,*
> *Find someone who has achieved the results you want*
> *And copy what they do*
> *And you'll achieve the same results".*
> **Tony Robbins**.

Women may share a lot of things (the blogosphere explosion is a testament to this) but having a strong mentor usually is not one, men seem to be more apt at networking with purpose and connecting with people who can help them rather than just sharing experiences.

Having a mentor is one the most critical factors for continuous growth and accelerated success.

Picking both men and women mentors that tell you not what you want to hear but what you need to hear is priceless: men will give you an insight in the way things are (if we are to believe the *"old boys club"* exists) and they can be an inside ally and advocate.

Women can guide you on potential obstacles they faced specifically as female and how they dealt with them.

• • •

Action point

I'm not going to make assumptions so I'm going to ask you outright: do you have a mentor (or hopefully more)? If not, why not? If yes, how have they helped you so far?

....
....
....
....
....
....
....
....
....

...

With your map in mind, thinking about your strengths and weaknesses, what other/additional mentors might you need in the future? (If you have already someone, don't feel like you are being disloyal — it is not just OK to have different mentors for different things, it is highly recommended).

....
....
....
....
....
....
....
....
....
....
....
....
....
....
....

Think of specific examples of support/guidance that you need and the type of mentor that would fulfill your need (their background/experience , etc.).

. . . .

. . . .

. . . .

. . . .

. . . .

. . . .

. . . .

. . . .

. . . .

. . . .

. . . .

. . . .

. . . .

. . . .

. . . .

. . . .

. . . .

. . . .

. . . .

. . . .

. . . .

. . . .

. . . .

. . . .

. . . .

3 things to be thankful for

Think back at the topic covered today — what are the 3 things you are grateful for, despite everything? Remember, if you can't think of any — you are not looking hard enough. Think again.

....
....
....
....
....
....
....
....
....
....
....
....
....
....
....
....
....
....
....
....
....
....
....
....
....
....

DAY 25: THINK OUTSIDE THE BOX: WHAT BOX? THINK THE PART

The Monkey Mind/dump the c*** exercise

P **rompt:**
    Modeling

....
....
....
....
....
....
....
....
....
....
....
....
....
....

Mirror Mirror

Mirror, Mirror refers to the NeuroLinguistic Programming technique of Mirroring and Matching to build rapport.

Mirroring is one of the most useful NLP techniques there are, is innate and even chimps use mirroring within their groups.

It is useful to determine whether people are visual, audial, or kinaesthetic (you do so by listening to their language patterns) and consequently adapt your presentation and communication/language style to suit the specific audience and have more impact.

State	Primary sense	Language patterns
Visual	Sight	I see; it looks good
Audial	Hearing	Sounds good; that rings a bell
Kinaesthetic	Feeling	That doesn't feel right; I can't put my finger on it

Conscious and deliberate use of mirroring can also help to break down barriers, in negotiations, meetings, new environments, interviews , etc.

Action point

Look back at the exercises you have done so far: what are the language patterns that you have used primarily throughout?

....
....
....
....
....
....
....
....

What those language patterns correspond to: Visual, Audial or Kinaesthetic? Is that what you thought, believed you were?

....
....
....
....
....
....
....
....
....

Mirror and Match practice = identify three key people in your next level peer group that display the required thinking levels you have previously identified as needed to move you forward. Start to Mirror and Match (be careful not to come across as parroting).

. . .

It would be useful to start with people that have the same language patterns you have (e.g., Visual/Audial/Kinaesthetic) — this will make it much easier and look much more natural.

....
....
....
....
....
....
....
....
....
....
....
....
....
....
....

Plan situations when you can carefully listen (to their thinking process) and observe this is put across (language patterns). Schedule.

....
....
....
....
....
....
....
....
....
....
....
....
....

Mirror and Match practice = identify three other people in your next level group that display the required thinking levels (as previous exercise) but this time with people that have the other two language patterns. Same "thinking levels," different ways of expressing; this will expand your tool kit.

....
....
....
....
....
....
....
....
....
....
....
....
....

As previously, plan situations and schedule them.

....
....
....
....
....
....
....
....
....
....
....
....
....
....
....

3 things to be thankful for

Think back at the topic covered today — what are the 3 things you are grateful for, despite everything? Remember, if you can't think of any — you are not looking hard enough. Think again.

....
....
....
....
....
....
....
....
....
....
....
....
....
....
....
....
....
....
....
....
....
....
....
....
....

DAY 26: THINK OUTSIDE THE BOX: WHAT BOX? THINK THE PART

The Monkey Mind/dump the c*** exercise

P **rompt:**
   Mindset

....

....

....

....

....

....

....

....

....

....

....

....

....

....

More Mirror work

As I mentioned yesterday, it is useful to determine whether people are visual, audial, or kinaesthetic (you do so by listening to their language patterns) and consequently adapt your presentation and communication/language style to suit the specific audience and have more impact.

State	Primary sense	Language patterns
Visual	Sight	I see; it looks good
Audial	Hearing	Sounds good; that rings a bell
Kinaesthetic	Feeling	That doesn't feel right; I can't put my finger on it

Action point

Now that you have more awareness about yourself, let's look at your stakeholder map (just a fancy word to encompass all the people that have an interest in the output of your role/the projects you are working on). You should have carried out this exercise for the next level peer group yesterday. Today let's look at your boss and two other people in roles more senior than yours who are affected by your work: what are the language patterns that they use primarily in their communication?

....

....

....

....

....

....

....

....

What those language patterns correspond to: Visual, Audial or Kinaesthetic?

....
....
....
....
....
....
....
....
....
....

Mirror and Match practice (be careful not to come across as parroting). It would be useful to start with people that have the same language patterns you have (e.g., Visual/Audial/Kinaesthetic) — this will make it much easier and look much more natural and then move on.

Plan the occasions when you can start and schedule them.

....
....
....
....
....
....
....
....
....
....
....
....
....
....

Mirror and Match practice = identify three other people in the next level group but this time with people that have the other two language patterns.

Same "thinking levels," different ways of expressing; this will expand your tool kit.

....
....
....
....
....
....
....
....
....
....
....

Based on your findings, review any forthcoming communication you need to have and plan the discussion/presentation , etc., style to match their language pattern/s (you'll see — life will be soo much easier that way).

....
....
....
....
....
....
....
....
....
....
....
....
....
....
....

3 things to be thankful for

Think back at the topic covered today — what are the 3 things you are grateful for, despite everything? Remember, if you can't think of any — you are not looking hard enough. Think again.

....

....

....

....

....

....

....

....

....

....

....

....

....

....

....

....

....

....

....

....

....

....

....

....

....

....

....

DAY 27: THINK OUTSIDE THE BOX: WHAT BOX? THINK THE PART

The Monkey Mind/dump the c*** exercise

P**rompt:**
Role Models

....
....
....
....
....
....
....
....
....
....
....
....
....
....
....

The power of role models

In every story, every hero is helped through his/her journey when meeting a mentor and then allies along the way.

Virtual or "real" mentors/allies/role models to show you their "call to adventure", their crossing of thresholds together with perhaps tests, allies and maybe enemies.

Women can and should empower other women instead of throwing away "the ladder" after they climbed it.

Action point

Now let's go and find these women: look both in the public eye, in professional organizations, in your company and so on. Women who have done it and are living their life on their terms.

Look for women at different stages in their journey so, when you are feeling down and out, discouraged in some way, you also can get some inspiration and let it flow ...

I'm saying women specifically because they will understand first hand what it is like to be an ambitious woman in the workplace and the obstacles you are facing. They can also show you how they overcome those obstacles along the way.

Mentors can be both in person e.g. an actual relationship with regular meetings and/or virtual via books/podcasts/YouTube/Ted Talks , etc.

....

....

....
....
....
....
....
....
....
....
....
....
....
....

From the list, choose at least three and plan how you can make either contact and strike a relationship and/or, in case of virtual mentors, how can you target and maximize your learning from their offering.

....
....
....
....
....
....
....
....
....
....
....
....
....
....
....

Great job.

3 things to be thankful for

Think back at the topic covered today — what are the 3 things you are grateful for, despite everything? Remember, if you can't think of any — you are not looking hard enough. Think again.

....
....
....
....
....
....
....
....
....
....
....
....
....
....
....
....
....
....
....
....
....
....
....
....
....

DAY 28: REST, RELAXATION AND SOME REFLECTION

The Monkey Mind/dump the c*** exercise

P rompt:
Self-belief

....
....
....
....
....
....
....
....
....
....
....
....
....
....

This page is intentionally left blank

3 things to be thankful for

Think back at the topic covered today — what are the 3 things you are grateful for, despite everything? Remember, if you can't think of any — you are not looking hard enough. Think again.

....

....

....

....

....

....

....

....

....

....

....

....

....

....

....

....

....

....

....

....

....

....

....

....

....

....

DAY 29: REST, RELAXATION AND SOME REFLECTION

The Monkey Mind/dump the c*** exercise

P **rompt:**
  Empowerment

....
....
....
....
....
....
....
....
....
....
....
....
....
....

This page is intentionally left blank

3 things to be thankful for

Think back at the topic covered today — what are the 3 things you are grateful for, despite everything? Remember, if you can't think of any — you are not looking hard enough. Think again.

....
....
....
....
....
....
....
....
....
....
....
....
....
....
....
....
....
....
....
....
....
....
....
....
....
....

DAY 30: RECAP

The Monkey Mind/dump the c*** exercise

Prompt:
  Future

....
....
....
....
....
....
....
....
....
....
....
....
....
....

All together now

Now is the time to look back at the journey for the past 30 days, make some decisions and plan your way forward.

Action point

Describe your journey for the past 30 days — the good, the bad and the ugly.

....
....
....
....
....
....
....
....
....
....
....
....
....
....

What was the lowest point and why?

....
....
....
....
....
....
....
....

What was the highest point and why?

....
....
....
....
....
....
....
....

What have you learned about yourself?

....
....
....
....
....
....
....
....
....

What do you really (REALLY) want to achieve — the ultimate goal?

....
....
....
....
....
....
....
....
....
....
....

Why do you want it? What will give you?

....
....
....
....
....
....
....
....

What is your definition of success?

....
....
....
....
....
....
....
....

What price, if any, are you willing to pay?

....
....
....
....
....
....
....
....
....
....
....
....

What are the barriers you are facing to achieve your goal and how are you going to tackle them now?

....
....
....
....
....
....
....
....

Career mapping: your next role toward the ultimate goal (if not the same).

....
....
....
....
....
....
....

List three different levels of thinking identified in the next role and how you can start applying them in 1) the YOU Plc.; 2) in your current role.

....
....
....
....
....
....
....
....
....

Identify the next level up peer group and the steps you are going to take to make contact with them.

....
....
....
....
....
....
....
....
....

Identify three role models/mentors and the steps you are going to take to start the mentor/mentee relationship.

....
....
....
....
....
....
....
....

Plan and schedule appropriate occasions for you to start practicing to Mirror and Match (Visual, Audial and Kinaesthetic).

....
....
....
....
....
....
....
....

3 things to be thankful for

Think back at the topic covered today — what are the 3 things you are grateful for, despite everything? Remember, if you can't think of any — you are not looking hard enough. Think again.

....
....
....
....
....
....
....
....
....
....
....
....
....
....
....
....
....
....
....
....
....
....
....
....
....

LOOK THE PART

30 DAYS TO REBOOT YOUR BRAND

DAY 31: THERE IS NOTHING TO FEAR BUT FEAR ITSELF

The Monkey Mind/dump the c*** exercise

Prompt:
What comes to mind when thinking of the words 'my image'?

....
....
....
....
....
....
....
....
....
....
....
....
....
....
....
....

The fear process

Yes, it is time for the fear process again. It is one of the most powerful I have ever encountered; I do it and re-do it again each time I start a new project/venture (including this book), both in my professional and personal life. It is not going to kill you to do it again.

Fear contributes to self-sabotage; it keeps us from extending ourselves and taking chances. So we need to bring it (or them) to the open. Face your fear/s.

"Fear is the mind-killer" - Frank Herbert.

Ready?

Ok, ready or not, here it is — trust me, it is necessary to go through this (and NO cheating - do not skip it - you'll thank me later).

A quick reminder on how the process works:

A fear I have about .... is that ....

1 If you don't think you have fears about rebooting your image to support your career goal, you KNOW you are lying to yourself. But let's pretend for a minute you don't have any, or you run out of them, make something up — even if you think they are totally fabricated (your subconscious mind will tell you, believe me).

    2 Do not judge. If something comes up, don't try to deduce what it means and if it applies to you. Write it down anyway.

3 If a thought arises that is so upsetting that you are uncomfortable writing it down, write it down anyway!

4 Don't edit your thoughts. And don't waste any time trying to justify what you are writing, telling yourself it is not important and that's not how you really feel. And don't get entangled with thinking that writing your fears down will make them real, either. The purpose of this process is to let go of your fears, and you can do so by discharging them from your mind onto the page.

Write as fast as possible, following the process. Write down at least a full page. Minimum.

Before you start, think about what brought you here, your professional situation and what you are trying to achieve.

BREATHE.

Breathe again.

Turn the page and start the process.

Go ahead.

A fear I have about rebooting my professional and personal image is that

....
....
....
....
....
....
....
....
....
....
....
....
....
....
....
....
....
....
....
....
....
....
....
....
....
....
....
....
....
....
....

Take a moment to write down more things that fear has kept you from doing throughout your career.

....
....
....
....
....
....
....
....
....
....
....
....
....
....
....
....
....
....
....
....
....
....
....
....
....
....
....
....
....
....

Done?

And now, to move on from here write the following:

"I am willing to act in the presence of fear. I hereby resolve for the next 60 days to commit and continue this journey and that I will not allow fear to keep me from doing something I genuinely desire to do".

Then sign your name and date it.

Name ....

Date ....

Enough for today — good job!

3 things to be thankful for

Think back at the topic covered today — what are the 3 things you are grateful for, despite everything? Remember, if you can't think of any — you are not looking hard enough. Think again.

....
....
....
....
....
....
....
....
....
....
....
....
....
....
....
....
....
....
....
....
....
....
....
....
....
....

You see? It wasn't that difficult, was it? Great work.

DAY 32: WHERE ARE YOU NOW?

The Monkey Mind/dump the c*** exercise

P **rompt:**
   What comes to mind when thinking of diversity and branding?

....
....
....
....
....
....
....
....
....
....
....
....
....
....

The Overview

We discussed on day two how boardroom diversity is increasing, although women remain underrepresented.

Research from many worldwide organizations has found that three women or more are needed to create a "critical mass," leading to better financial performance, yet only 20.1% have at least three women.

MSCI found that having three or more women changes the boardroom dynamics and "enhances the likelihood that women's voices and ideas are heard, " resulting in better financial results.

They also found that companies with fewer women on boards had more governance-related controversies than average.

Action Point

On day two, you researched and raised your awareness on this subject, gathered information about your customers, markets, demographics and compared the male to female ratio of your sector/customer base to the company you work for. In addition, you should have also ascertained the number of females in middle management and leadership positions compared to males in the same position.

Now that you have all this information, it is time to explore further.

Can your company image be matched with your products?

....
....
....
....
....

Does your company image resonate with your target audience?

....
....
....
....
....

What effect does your company's corporate image have on its reputation?

....
....
....
....
....

In your opinion, where are the gaps?

....
....
....
....
....

Do you have any suggestions for improving your company image?

....
....
....
....

Now think about males and females in leadership positions (especially in externally facing roles); how well do they represent the company's brand image?

....
....
....
....
....
....
....
....
....
....

A Brand promise encourages customers to remember what the company brand stands for. It's all about the presentation to create the right impression. How well does their image represent the diversity of your customers, your company staff makeup and your company brand image?

....
....
....
....
....
....
....
....
....
....
....
....
....
....
....
....

UN Women "Roadmap for Substantive Equality: 2030" aims to repeal and amend discriminatory laws against women whilst ensuring that regulations are supportive in general of gender equality & women's human rights.

The UN Women Roadmap for Substantive Equality: 2030 focuses not only on achieving legislative reform but equally, and more crucially, that they are put into practice.

Gender-discriminatory laws are often rooted in discriminatory social norms, which remain pervasive and are difficult to change.

Action Point

List current dress code norms you believe to be discriminatory.

....
....
....
....
....
....
....
....
....
....
....
....
....
....
....
....

Great job!

3 things to be thankful for

Think back at the topic covered today — what are the 3 things you are grateful for, despite everything? Remember, if you can't think of any — you are not looking hard enough. Think again.

....
....
....
....
....
....
....
....
....
....
....
....
....
....
....
....
....
....
....
....
....
....
....
....
....
....
....

DAY 33: ONCE UPON A TIME

The Monkey Mind/dump the c*** exercise

Prompt:
What is a woman's place? And what is her image?

....
....
....
....
....
....
....
....
....
....
....
....
....
....

A woman's place

We have seen previously what a "woman's place" is or seen to be has varied throughout history from warriors, powerful priestesses, and political leaders to portrayals inferior to men. Looking at the position of women at different points in history can show us how our society has grown and changed and help us understand the present, including barriers.

Women have gained and lost power at different times in history; they have been painted and portrayed beautifully whilst not affecting their lives on a day-to-day basis, aka a woman's place was the homemaker.

The most significant gains inequality had to wait until the twentieth century, for example, with the Suffragettes' successful campaign for women being granted the right to vote. World War I and II also showed that women could contribute to the economy and work both inside and outside the home, taking men's places in factories.

The sixties and seventies and the advent of feminism further changed some of society's perceptions and, most importantly, changed women's own beliefs.

Action point

On day three, you looked back at three specific times in history of your choice and a woman's place in those times. What were women expected to look like in those times?

....

....

....

....

....

....

....
....
....
....
....
....
....
....
....

How was the image expectation reflective of women's role in society in those three times?

....
....
....
....
....

What was different in the image of the three heroines you identified from the expected image:

....
....
....
....
....
....
....
....

What was aligned ? And what wasn't?

....
....
....
....
....
....
....
....
....
....
....
....
....
....
....
....
....
....
....
....
....
....
....
....
....
....
....
....
....

Shorter day today, good job.

3 things to be thankful for

Think back at the topic covered today — what are the 3 things you are grateful for, despite everything? Remember, if you can't think of any — you are not looking hard enough. Think again.

....
....
....
....
....
....
....
....
....
....
....
....
....
....
....
....
....
....
....
....
....
....
....
....
....

DAY 34: WHAT ARE YOUR BARRIERS - PART 1

The Monkey Mind/dump the c*** exercise

P **rompt:**
    What comes to mind when you hear the word barrier?

....
....
....
....
....
....
....
....
....
....
....
....
....
....

Cultural, religious & family paradigms

Religion is a controversial topic: it is difficult to talk about it without insulting/annoying someone somewhere and without being disputed on the interpretation/misinterpretation of the scripture/s.

However, religion has played/is playing and will continue to play a big part in the way different groups of people perceive themselves and others and their definition of "what good looks like," including women and their role in society and that there is a correlation between the two.

Many religions share the same characterizations and expectations of a traditional female role, gender and sexual identity, and unique image expectations that determine what you believe you can and cannot do, how you should do it, and why and how you should look and why.

Action Point

What effect do you think your cultural background, religion, and family paradigms had on building your image/look, including what you considerable 'appropriate' and how have they limited you — if they did, that is.

....
....
....
....
....
....
....
....
....
....
....
....

....
....
....
....
....
....
....
....
....
....
....
....

What are your inherited views about how mothers should look like? What is no longer appropriate to wear once you are a mother?

....
....
....
....
....
....
....
....
....
....
....
....
....
....
....
....
....
....

How did these share your current personal and professional image?

....
....
....
....
....
....
....
....
....
....
....
....
....
....
....
....
....
....
....
....
....
....
....
....
....
....
....

Gosh, that was heavy - You need a break for today.

3 things to be thankful for

Think back at the topic covered today — what are the 3 things you are grateful for, despite everything? Remember, if you can't think of any — you are not looking hard enough. Think again.

....

....

....

....

....

....

....

....

....

....

....

....

....

....

....

....

....

....

....

....

....

....

....

....

....

....

DAY 35: WHAT ARE YOUR BARRIERS - PART 2

The Monkey Mind/dump the c*** exercise

P **rompt:**
   What comes to mind when you hear the words "good girl"? Is she pretty?

....
....
....
....
....
....
....
....
....
....
....
....
....
....

The "good girl syndrome"

Although there is definitely the outer game of society/family para-digms and so on, there is also a far more important inner game, your own perceptions, your own decisions, belief systems that drive behavior and choices made — the "good girl syndrome".

Rachida Dati comes to mind, the French Justice Minister under French President Nicolas Sarkozy who went back to work five days after having her first child by Caesarean section. Seeing her going back as what is perceived (by whom?) too soon started a barrage and ping-pong of comments and articles, some quite bitching and derogative and some alleging bullying from Sarkozy (and the worse ones were from women).

Even the way she was described ("impossibly glamorous and thin") had negative connotations (like what-all new mothers must look/are fat and frumpy??).

Better still, people were discussing if she is *"right to put the demands of her career ahead of her child? Or is she crazy to miss out on some of the most precious months of her life? "* like there is only one way of being a mother AND a career woman at the same time.

Action Point

How much have your cultural/religious and family paradigms conditioned your views on what is "good girl" 's image?

....
....
....

How much has it affected your personal and professional image and outfit choice?

....
....
....
....
....
....
....
....
....
....
....
....
....
....
....
....
....
....
....
....
....
....
....
....
....

Short day today — great job.

3 things to be thankful for

Think back at the topic covered today — what are the 3 things you are grateful for, despite everything? Remember, if you can't think of any — you are not looking hard enough. Think again.

....
....
....
....
....
....
....
....
....
....
....
....
....
....
....
....
....
....
....
....
....
....
....
....
....
....
....

DAY 36: WHAT ARE YOUR BARRIERS - PART 3

The Monkey Mind/dump the c*** exercise

P**rompt:**
   What comes to mind when you hear the words age body "bias"?

....
....
....
....
....
....
....
....
....
....
....
....
....
....

Who's a "good girl"?

Today we are going to delve even deeper and this time into "your" idea of a "good girl".

Action point

You should now have a good idea of your beliefs derived from the social/religious and family paradigms regarding the "good girl" syndrome and the impact on your current image, both personal and professional.

Now think back at times when you applied this "learnt judgement" and passed it onto others: go as far back or as near as you need to. Actually, I invite you to do so on purpose and see how and if your views changed with time.

Describe three different occasions at three different times in your life when you have demonstrated bias towards other women's image/looks — or yourself — based on the learnt "good girl" syndrome belief (it is hard to admit, but we all do it and we all project our beliefs with our behavior — the point here is to have awareness).

....
....
....
....
....
....
....
....
....
....
....
....
....
....

....
....
....
....
....
....
....
....
....
....
....

How would you/could behave differently now, if the same situations arise again?

....
....
....
....
....
....
....
....
....
....
....
....

With understanding and acknowledging your own biases, you are taking step forward to a more level playing field — for yourself and other women. Congratulations.

3 things to be thankful for

Think back at the topic covered today — what are the 3 things you are grateful for, despite everything? Remember, if you can't think of any — you are not looking hard enough. Think again.

....
....
....
....
....
....
....
....
....
....
....
....
....
....
....
....
....
....
....
....
....
....
....
....
....

DAY 37: REST, RELAXATION AND SOME REFLECTION

The Monkey Mind/dump the c*** exercise

P rompt:
Self-image

....
....
....
....
....
....
....
....
....
....
....
....
....
....

This page is intentionally left blank

3 things to be thankful for

Think back at the topic covered today — what are the 3 things you are grateful for, despite everything? Remember, if you can't think of any — you are not looking hard enough. Think again.

....
....
....
....
....
....
....
....
....
....
....
....
....
....
....
....
....
....
....
....
....
....
....
....
....

DAY 38: REST, RELAXATION AND SOME REFLECTION

The Monkey Mind/dump the c*** exercise

P**rompt:**
    Time for self care

....
....
....
....
....
....
....
....
....
....
....
....
....

This page is intentionally left blank

3 things to be thankful for

Think back at the topic covered today — what are the 3 things you are grateful for, despite everything? Remember, if you can't think of any — you are not looking hard enough. Think again.

....
....
....
....
....
....
....
....
....
....
....
....
....
....
....
....
....
....
....
....
....
....
....
....
....
....
....

DAY 39: SUCCESS IS A RELATIVE THING - PART 1

*The Monkey Mind/dump the c*** exercise*

P**rompt:**
    What comes to mind when you hear the word SUCCESSFUL brand?

....
....
....
....
....
....
....
....
....
....
....
....
....
....
....

What does successful branding mean to you?

Success means so many things to so many people; if you don't define what good (or great) looks like, you will be always chasing something, the next shiny object, unachievable targets and never be quite satisfied. This is applicable to your "brand" image too.

Action Point

Pause for a minute and think — jot down what is your definition of a successful brand image.

....
....
....
....
....
....
....
....

Where does this definition originate from (family, friends, peers)?

....
....
....
....
....
....
....
....

Is this definition still relevant to you now? If yes (or no), why yes (or no)?

....
....
....
....
....
....
....

Has this definition changed in the last few years? If yes, what has changed?

....
....
....
....
....
....
....

What has been the constant (as compared to the variable) in your definition of successful (brand) image?

....
....
....
....
....
....

Well done.

3 things to be thankful for

Think back at the topic covered today — what are the 3 things you are grateful for, despite everything? Remember, if you can't think of any — you are not looking hard enough. Think again.

....

....

....

....

....

....

....

....

....

....

....

....

....

....

....

....

....

....

....

....

....

....

....

....

....

DAY 40: SUCCESS IS A RELATIVE THING - PART 2

The Monkey Mind/dump the c*** exercise

P rompt:
    What do you feel when you hear the words YOU DON'T FIT?

....
....
....
....
....
....
....
....
....
....
....
....
....
....

What does success really really mean to you?

Success means so many things to so many people; we have looked at what is your definition of success and how that has changed from a rational viewpoint. Now is the time to go deeper into your feelings.

NO, DEEPER.

Action point

Take some time to think about what success really means to you: a job well done? Position? Power? How do really successful people look like?

....
....
....
....
....
....
....
....
....
....
....
....
....
....
....
....
....
....
....
....
....
....

How has your personal image impacted your confidence to achieve your desired result?

....
....
....
....
....
....
....

What actions have you already taken regarding your professional image if any?

....
....
....
....
....
....
....
....
....

Is your current image a good "vehicle" for your destination? If not, why not? If yes, how?

....
....
....
....
....
....
....
....

What makes you really happy about your current image?

....
....
....
....
....
....
....
....
....
....
....
....
....
....
....
....
....
....
....
....
....
....
....

Great job.

3 things to be thankful for

Think back at the topic covered today — what are the 3 things you are grateful for, despite everything? Remember, if you can't think of any — you are not looking hard enough. Think again.

....
....
....
....
....
....
....
....
....
....
....
....
....
....
....
....
....
....
....
....
....
....
....
....
....

DAY 41: WHAT IS YOUR WHY?

The Monkey Mind/dump the c*** exercise

P **rompt:**
Who do you want to be? How do you want to be perceived?

....
....
....
....
....
....
....
....
....
....
....
....
....
....

The Maslow Hierarchy of Needs

We have talked previously about Maslow's Hierarchy of Needs, one of the best-known motivational theories trying to understand what drives "humans".

As a reminder, Maslow suggests that people are motivated to fulfill basic needs before moving on to the more advanced needs, trying to understand what makes people happy and what they do/would do to meet their needs. He believed that people have an innate need and desire to be all they can be, but to do so, they must meet first several more basic needs.

According to Maslow, there are five different levels starting at the lowest, known as physiological needs.

Growth needs are at the highest levels of the pyramid, which do not stem from deprivation but rather from a desire to grow as a person.

The need for security and safety becomes primary, and it is all about control and order in our lives and consequent behaviors (financial security, health and wellness, protection against accidents and injury).

The need for appreciation and respect, e.g., gaining the respect and appreciation of others, leads to the need to accomplish things and then have efforts recognized together with the feeling of accomplishment and prestige, self-esteem and personal worth.

Self-actualization - "What a man can be, he must be" is the need people have to achieve their full potential as human beings.

Similarly to Maslow, Tony Robbins talks about the same drivers of human behaviors in a more fluid way:
- Certainty and security
- Uncertainty and variety
- Significance

- Love & Connection
- Growth
- Contribution.

It is essential to understand that basic human needs need to be fulfilled on top of the infrastructural belief system based on cultural, religious (or non-religious) & family paradigms.

Action Point

This is a good time for a pause and to reflect: which need/s is/are the most important to you right now? Certainty? Variety? Significance? Love & connection ? Or growth & contribution?

Why is that?

....
....
....
....
....
....
....
....
....
....
....
....
....
....
....
....

What need/s are you trying to satisfy in the way you are portraying yourself/your image? (In these 30 days we are working on Looking The Part, remember?)

....
....
....
....
....
....
....
....
....
....
....
....
....
....

Refer back to your definition of how success looks like — are you matching that description?

....
....
....
....
....
....
....
....
....
....
....

You are doing great.

3 things to be thankful for

Think back at the topic covered today — what are the 3 things you are grateful for, despite everything? Remember, if you can't think of any — you are not looking hard enough. Think again.

....

....

....

....

....

....

....

....

....

....

....

....

....

....

....

....

....

....

....

....

....

....

....

....

....

....

DAY 42: WHAT IS THE PRICE?

*The Monkey Mind/dump the c*** exercise*

Prompt:
   Have you paid a price?

....
....
....
....
....
....
....
....
....
....
....
....
....
....

Everyone pays a price

There is a perception that women (even more so women with children) pay a price to rise to the top of an organization/field , etc., (as opposed to it is easy for men?).

Let's face it:

Leadership requires 100% commitment – Everyone pays a price.
But what about when it comes to image in leadership position?

Action Point

We talked previously that, if the "price to pay" for success/the position is perceived as "too big/painful" and/or unfair, there will always be an invisible barrier, like a force field stopping you from getting there.

Is there an additional price for women to pay, e.g., forgo their femininity for example, and become "male clones"? What are your views on this?

....
....
....
....
....
....
....
....
....
....
....
....
....
....
....

In the 2015 Global Entrepreneurship Monitor (GEM) Special Report on Women Entrepreneurship, women's entrepreneurship rose by 6% world-wide in the last two years.

According to the 2016 Kauffman Index of Start-up Activity, in the United States women make up 40% of new entrepreneurs (highest since 1996). In the MasterCard Index of Women Entrepreneurs 2017 (MIWE) women's business ownership across the 54 markets measured make up between 25-35% of total business owners.

Action Point

Check out profiles on LinkedIn and females leaders in Trade magazines or magazines in general: is there a difference between the image of Female CEOs of big corporations and Female Founders? What are the difference? BE specific, it will be useful later on.

....
....
....
....
....
....
....
....
....
....
....
....
....
....
....

3 things to be thankful for

Think back at the topic covered today — what are the 3 things you are grateful for, despite everything? Remember, if you can't think of any — you are not looking hard enough. Think again.

....
....
....
....
....
....
....
....
....
....
....
....
....
....
....
....
....
....
....
....
....
....
....
....
....
....

DAY 43: PERFECTION IS BORING - BE AWESOME INSTEAD

The Monkey Mind/dump the c*** exercise

P rompt:
   What comes to mind when thinking of perfect image?

....
....
....
....
....
....
....
....
....
....
....
....
....
....

Wonder Woman does not exist

I'll repeat it again. The idea that you should take as little maternity leave as possible, work until your waters break beneath your desk, never complain of sickness, swollen ankles and/or backache, and then go back to work fast and/or go back to work and (as much as you love your baby and being a mum) enjoying being back to work and more than baby-talk, but feeling guilty all the way through it, and then coming back home and be the "perfect" wife/partner/significant other (whatever you like to be called) and cooking, cleaning, tidying and putting the baby to bed is ludicrous.

Silence your inner critic — do you and what works for you.
And this includes your individuality and image.

Action Point

Does the picture described above sound like someone you know? Maybe intimately? What are the things that you do to please your inner critic? Has anything changed in the last 30 days?

....
....
....
....
....
....
....
....
....
....
....
....
....
....

3 things to be thankful for

Think back at the topic covered today — what are the 3 things you are grateful for, despite everything? Remember, if you can't think of any — you are not looking hard enough. Think again.

....
....
....
....
....
....
....
....
....
....
....
....
....
....
....
....
....
....
....
....
....
....
....
....
....
....

DAY 44: REST, RELAXATION AND SOME REFLECTION

The Monkey Mind/dump the c*** exercise

P **rompt:**
    Forgiveness of your flaws

....
....
....
....
....
....
....
....
....
....
....
....
....
....
....

This page is intentionally left blank

3 things to be thankful for

Think back at the topic covered today — what are the 3 things you are grateful for, despite everything? Remember, if you can't think of any — you are not looking hard enough. Think again.

....
....
....
....
....
....
....
....
....
....
....
....
....
....
....
....
....
....
....
....
....
....
....
....
....
....
....

DAY 45: REST, RELAXATION AND SOME REFLECTION

The Monkey Mind/dump the c*** exercise

P rompt:
Self-esteem

....
....
....
....
....
....
....
....
....
....
....
....
....
....
....

This page is intentionally left blank

3 things to be thankful for

Think back at the topic covered today — what are the 3 things you are grateful for, despite everything? Remember, if you can't think of any — you are not looking hard enough. Think again.

....
....
....
....
....
....
....
....
....
....
....
....
....
....
....
....
....
....
....
....
....
....
....
....
....

DAY 46: THINK OUTSIDE THE BOX: WHAT BOX? LOOK THE PART

The Monkey Mind/dump the c*** exercise

P **rompt:**
   First Impressions

....
....
....
....
....
....
....
....
....
....
....
....
....
....

The power of first impressions

According to Malcolm Gladwell, in "Blink: The Power of Thinking Without Thinking" people make up their minds about people they meet for the first time instantaneously or in two-seconds — can you imagine?!

Research also suggests that first impressions can be so powerful that they can become more important and believable than fact.

Recent studies presented at the Society of Personality and Social Psychology annual conference in Texas found that even when told whether a person was gay or straight, people identified a person's sexual orientation based on how they looked — irrespectively of the facts blatantly contradicting their impression.

"We judge books by their covers, and we can't help but do it," said Nicholas Rule, PhD, of the University of Toronto. "With effort, we can overcome this to some extent, but we are continually tasked with needing to correct ourselves.

Furthermore, the less time we have to make our judgments, the more likely we are to go with our gut, even over fact.

As soon as one sees another person, an impression is formed. This happens so quickly that what we see can sometimes dominate what we know," Rule said.

Additionally, the first impression formed online is often more negative than a first impression formed in person.

· · ·

Action point

Think back at least two occasions when you made assumptions about people you had just met based on their appearance: let's start with your private life.

....
....
....
....
....
....
....
....
....
....
....
....
....
....
....

How did you behave with those people based on your initial assumptions?

....
....
....
....
....
....
....
....
....
....
....
....
....
....

Did your behavior change once you got to know them? How?

....
....
....
....
....
....
....
....
....
....
....
....
....
....

Now let's repeat exactly the full exercise with your professional life. If you think you have never done so, think again — we ALL do it and so have you.

....
....
....
....
....
....
....
....
....
....
....
....
....
....
....

Ok, to finish for the day, let's look back when other people have made assumptions about yourself and treated you a certain way (which?) because of those assumptions (pick an example from your personal life or professional life — either, both and go as deep as you wish). How did it make you feel?

....

....

....

....

....

....

....

....

....

....

....

....

....

....

....

....

....

....

....

....

....

....

....

....

....

....

....

....

....

Can you recognize where these biases are coming from? Might be worth revisiting previous week/s exercises here, just saying ;-)...

....
....
....
....
....
....
....
....
....
....
....
....
....
....
....
....
....
....
....
....
....
....
....
....
....
....
....
....

Great job.

3 things to be thankful for

Think back at the topic covered today — what are the 3 things you are grateful for, despite everything? Remember, if you can't think of any — you are not looking hard enough. Think again.

....

....

....

....

....

....

....

....

....

....

....

....

....

....

....

....

....

....

....

....

....

....

....

....

....

DAY 47: THINK OUTSIDE THE BOX: WHAT BOX? LOOK THE PART

The Monkey Mind/dump the c*** exercise

P **rompt:**
   Perceptions

....
....
....
....
....
....
....
....
....
....
....
....
....
....

The Halo effect

First impressions do matter for both good and bad depending if the first meeting was fine or not — positive = social cohesion; negative = potential biases and social prejudice — like a halo effect.

Our appearance makes an instant statement to others about who we are and what we are about.

I know that, when this subject is approached, women especially get all uppity saying appearance doesn't matter, shouldn't matter, blah blah blah …

I get it. It shouldn't. It does.

Additionally, the impression created by appearance further influences our judgement, creating the so-called halo effect.

What is the halo effect then?

It is a cognitive bias whereby the overall impression we have of a person affects how we feel and think about their character, e.g., you see someone in a similar light of your perception of one characteristic for all others.

For example, in a work setting, the halo effect is one of the most common biases affecting performance appraisals and reviews.

It also has an impact on how severely or lightly we perceive and judge mistakes.

For example, when someone that we perceive to be a "good guy / girl" makes a mistake, we tend to minimize the error "it's a one off"; "he / she might be going through something …".

On the contrary, when someone that we perceive as "not good" makes an error, then boy oh boy, " he / she always makes mistakes," "again? I knew it…" and so on.

Action point

Go back to the exercises done yesterday now: did those initial impressions in your private life create a halo effect in consequent interactions? If yes, how? Describe what happened. If not, are you sure, really sure? I thought so.

....
....
....
....
....
....
....
....
....
....
....
....
....
....
....
....
....
....
....
....
....
....
....
....
....
....
....
....
....
....
....
....
....
....
....

Now think back to examples when you have "applied" the halo effect in the workplace based on your perceptions and over-reacted or under-reacted to people based on this. Positive examples first: when did you underplay work errors/mistakes because of your overall opinion of the person/s? Be honest here.

....
....
....
....
....
....
....
....
....
....
....
....
....
....
....
....
....
....
....
....
....
....
....
....
....
....
....
....
....
....
....
....
....

Ok, now negative examples, when you overreacted to errors/mistakes (which you wouldn't have if the same errors came from "the good people"). Don't beat yourself up, we all do it. Recognizing own biases is the first step to beat them.

....
....
....
....
....
....
....
....
....
....
....
....
....
....
....
....
....
....
....
....
....
....
....
....
....

Great job.

3 things to be thankful for

Think back at the topic covered today — what are the 3 things you are grateful for, despite everything? Remember, if you can't think of any — you are not looking hard enough. Think again.

....

....

....

....

....

....

....

....

....

....

....

....

....

....

....

....

....

....

....

....

....

....

....

....

....

....

....

....

DAY 48: THINK OUTSIDE THE BOX: WHAT BOX? LOOK THE PART

The Monkey Mind/dump the c*** exercise

P rompt:
Snob

....
....
....
....
....
....
....
....
....
....
....
....
....

A book and its cover

Appearance does matter and it does with people in the same way that it does with products.

Manufacturing is one very good example of this.

Many times factories produce consumer goods that have the exact same recipe/product specification but, at the end of the production line, different labels are applied.

The products are then perceived/received in a completely different manner by consumers (including sometimes a substantial price point difference).

This is both because of the perception of quality (based on the branding/marketing of the different labels/brands) but also what buying certain brands says about us and how we want to be seen.

Think about that.

Action point

Make a list of the places where you habitually shop: what are the key components of their brand? What do they have in common?

....
....
....
....
....
....
....
....
....
....
....
....
....
....
....

Why do you shop there, be specific. What does it say about you as a consumer and as a person? How does that make you feel?

....
....
....
....
....
....
....
....
....
....
....
....
....

List all the shops you'd never be seen dead in: why is that? What are your associations with those brands? What do you think it says about people who shop there? Honesty is the key here — this is your workbook and nobody will see it unless you share it — challenge your perceptions.

....
....
....
....
....
....
....
....
....
....
....
....
....
....

Let's talk products now: are there any brands that you are particularly attached to — emotionally? Why are you attached to them?

....
....
....
....
....
....
....
....
....
....
....
....

I know right now you don't believe me, challenge yourself to carry out blind tests on five different types of products from branded houses and supermarket own labels. Make it a game with your friend and challenge your perceptions. Go on, you know you want to ...

What were the results?

....
....
....
....
....
....
....
....
....
....
....
....

Learned anything today then? I thought so ;-)

3 things to be thankful for

Think back at the topic covered today — what are the 3 things you are grateful for, despite everything? Remember, if you can't think of any — you are not looking hard enough. Think again.

....
....
....
....
....
....
....
....
....
....
....
....
....
....
....
....
....
....
....
....
....
....
....
....
....
....

DAY 49: THINK OUTSIDE THE BOX: WHAT BOX? LOOK THE PART

The Monkey Mind/dump the c*** exercise

P**rompt:**
Women in leadership

....
....
....
....
....
....
....
....
....
....
....
....
....
....

Leading Lady - Part 1

Personal style goes way beyond clothes and can also be used to communicate and reinforce your message.

> *"Style is a way to say who you are*
> *without having to speak,"*
> **- Rachel Zoe.**

Today we are going to, well actually you are going to, look into exactly this:

understanding what you are saying to the world.

Having knowledge about yourself and how you come across will enable you to create a personal style that goes beyond clothes and encompasses your approach to your career and life and how you feel about yourself.

Action Point

Describe your personal style — what are the words that come to mind?

....
....
....
....
....
....
....
....
....
....
....

What are the words that other people would use instead to describe your personal style? What do you think your style says about you? Are you aware of what are you projecting right now?

....
....
....
....
....
....
....
....
....
....
....
....
....

How does this contribute to the perception people might have of you (feel free to go back to previous days exercises if you need some help with this)?

....
....
....
....
....
....
....
....
....
....
....
....
....

How aligned is your current personal style to your career (and/or personal) aspirations?

....
....
....
....
....
....
....
....
....
....
....
....
....
....
....
....
....
....
....
....
....
....
....
....
....

Good job.

3 things to be thankful for

Think back at the topic covered today — what are the 3 things you are grateful for, despite everything? Remember, if you can't think of any — you are not looking hard enough. Think again.

....
....
....
....
....
....
....
....
....
....
....
....
....
....
....
....
....
....
....
....
....
....
....
....
....

DAY 50: THINK OUTSIDE THE BOX: WHAT BOX? LOOK THE PART

The Monkey Mind/dump the c*** exercise

P **rompt:**
  Fashion

....
....
....
....
....
....
....
....
....
....
....
....
....
....

Leading Lady - Part 2

> *"Real style is never right or wrong.*
> *It's a matter of being yourself on purpose."*
> **- G. Bruce Brier**

Personal style goes way beyond clothes and can also be used to communicate and reinforce your message.

Yesterday we looked at your current personal style and what your appearance says about you.

Today we are going to have some fun and create a Mood Board.

A **Mood Board** is a type of visual presentation or "collage" consisting of images, text, and samples of objects in a composition to convey a general idea or feeling about a particular topic. The topic, on this occasion, is the style of women you admire that appeal to you that you resonate with.

Action point

*Look at magazines, Pinterest, Instagram, or wherever you can find inspiration, and put together a so-called **Mood Board** for looks that you like.*

Personally I like physical things and keep them handy; you might want to do the same, as they'll be useful next week. I left a blank page so you can attach/pin "stuff". Have fun :-)

This page is intentionally left blank

3 things to be thankful for

Think back at the topic covered today — what are the 3 things you are grateful for, despite everything? Remember, if you can't think of any — you are not looking hard enough. Think again.

....
....
....
....
....
....
....
....
....
....
....
....
....
....
....
....
....
....
....
....
....
....
....
....
....

DAY 51: REST, RELAXATION AND SOME REFLECTION

The Monkey Mind/dump the c*** exercise

P **rompt:**
 Style

....
....
....
....
....
....
....
....
....
....
....
....
....
....

This page is intentionally left blank

3 things to be thankful for

Think back at the topic covered today — what are the 3 things you are grateful for, despite everything? Remember, if you can't think of any — you are not looking hard enough. Think again.

....
....
....
....
....
....
....
....
....
....
....
....
....
....
....
....
....
....
....
....
....
....
....
....
....
....
....

DAY 52: REST, RELAXATION AND SOME REFLECTION

The Monkey Mind/dump the c*** exercise

P**rompt:**
    My personal style

....
....
....
....
....
....
....
....
....
....
....
....
....
....

This page is intentionally left blank

3 things to be thankful for

Think back at the topic covered today — what are the 3 things you are grateful for, despite everything? Remember, if you can't think of any — you are not looking hard enough. Think again.

....
....
....
....
....
....
....
....
....
....
....
....
....
....
....
....
....
....
....
....
....
....
....
....
....
....

DAY 53: THINK OUTSIDE THE BOX: WHAT BOX? LOOK THE PART

The Monkey Mind/dump the c*** exercise

P rompt:
  Fashion icons

....
....
....
....
....
....
....
....
....
....
....
....
....
....

If you want to be the best, you need to learn from the best – I have not invented this phrase — you can hear it for the lips of the most successful entrepreneurs, CEOs, billionaires out there. And that is the point.

> *"If you want to be successful,*
> *find someone who has achieved the results you want*
> *and copy what they do*
> *and you'll achieve the same results,"*
> **- Tony Robbins.**

You need someone who has been there, seen it, done it and got the t-shirt so to speak and you can emulate exactly what he or she has done and shortcut your way to success.

This is applicable to both people you associate with on a daily basis and to choosing mentors to speed your journey, and includes the personal/work style department.

Today we are going to look at two fashion icons and how they used their personal style/appearance to communicate and reinforce their message: Jackie Kennedy Onassis and Diana, Princess of Wales.

I can picture your horrified faces right now reading this: Laura what? R-E-A-L-L-Y???

Yes, really (hey, I could have said the Queen, but that was pushing it a bit far perhaps …).

So, why Jackie Kennedy and Diana, Princess of Wales?

· · ·

Firstly, both women have been photographed ad infinitum and it will be easy for you to carry out the exercises.

Secondly, and most importantly, these are two women who were thrown into the public eye and have adapted their style to the specific situation to convey a message FOR that specific situation whilst remaining true to themselves and their "persona," on and off duty.

Two examples come to mind (but you can find endless):

- Jackie Kennedy wearing red, paying diplomatic tribute to the host country on her visit to Canada, and
- Diana wearing her "revenge" dress on the very night Prince Charles was making his adultery admission in a tell-all TV interview.

Diana evolved her style more and more through the years, and particularly so after her divorce, leaving beyond royal restrictions and protocols — a perfect example on how anyone can morph their style and re-invent themselves.

Both used clothes as self-expression and a means to communicate.
And so can you.

"Dress like you are going to meet
your worst enemy today"
- **Coco Chanel.**

Action point

Describe in your own words both women's style: what words come to mind and why?

....
....
....
....
....
....
....
....
....
....
....
....
....
....

How did they make people feel? Be specific: how, why...

....
....
....
....
....
....
....
....
....
....
....
....
....
....

Observe their style evolution throughout the years — what are the key points that stayed the same and what changed?

....
....
....
....
....
....
....
....
....
....
....
....
....
....

Pick three key pieces/looks for both women that were particularly significant for the purpose of the exercise, e.g., communicating through clothes: which one did you pick and why?

....
....
....
....
....
....
....
....
....
....
....
....
....
....

Think back at previous weeks' exercises: your definition of success and what it really means to you. Based on your answers, what does success physically look like for you (and I do mean visualize THAT image of success): what style/clothes do you associate it with?

....
....
....
....
....
....
....
....
....
....
....
....

What lessons can you apply to yourself from both women in creating an effective personal style aligned and supportive to your personal career ambitions/idea of success?

....
....
....
....
....
....
....
....
....
....
....
....

That's it for today, good job.

3 things to be thankful for

Think back at the topic covered today — what are the 3 things you are grateful for, despite everything? Remember, if you can't think of any — you are not looking hard enough. Think again.

....
....
....
....
....
....
....
....
....
....
....
....
....
....
....
....
....
....
....
....
....
....
....
....
....

DAY 54: THINK OUTSIDE THE BOX: WHAT BOX? LOOK THE PART

The Monkey Mind/dump the c*** exercise

P rompt:
Role models

....
....
....
....
....
....
....
....
....
....
....
....
....
....

In every story, every hero is helped through his/her journey when meeting a mentor and then allies along the way.

Virtual or "real" mentors/allies/role models to show you their "call to adventure', their crossing of thresholds together with perhaps tests, allies and maybe enemies.

In this case we are building from yesterday's exercises and looking at other successful women who can be your role model to bring to life the "Look The Part" methodology and help you along the way to create/evolve your personal style into your own personal armor to conquer your career (and personal) goals.

> *"Create your own style ... let it be unique for yourself*
> *and yet identifiable for others,"*
> - **Anna Wintour.**

Action point

Let's go and find these women: look both in the public eye, in professional organizations, in your company and so on. Women who have done it and are living their life on their terms whilst representing their company at the highest level.

....
....
....
....
....
....
....
....
....
....

From the list, choose at least three and plan how you can target and maxi-mize your learning — for example key looks during key moments in their career/for their company — how did they represent the company brand and assert themselves via their clothes/style?

....
....
....
....
....
....
....
....
....
....
....
....
....
....
....
....
....
....
....
....
....

"The process of growth,
of being an independent person,
of learning who you are and what you want from life,
is the real secret of life, happiness, and beauty …
A fulfilled woman is a beautiful woman,"
- Diane von Furstenberg.

3 things to be thankful for

Think back at the topic covered today — what are the 3 things you are grateful for, despite everything? Remember, if you can't think of any — you are not looking hard enough. Think again.

....
....
....
....
....
....
....
....
....
....
....
....
....
....
....
....
....
....
....
....
....
....
....
....
....
....
....
....

DAY 55: THINK OUTSIDE THE BOX: WHAT BOX? LOOK THE PART

The Monkey Mind/dump the c*** exercise

P**rompt:**
    Self-analysis

....
....
....
....
....
....
....
....
....
....
....
....
....
....

All together now

Now is the time to look back at the journey for the past few weeks, crystalize the learning so we can move into the fun part — building your new/evolved brand.

Action point

Describe your journey for the past three weeks — the good, the bad and the ugly.

....
....
....
....
....
....
....
....
....
....
....
....
....
....

What was the lowest point and why?

....
....
....
....
....
....

What was the highest point and why?

....
....
....
....
....
....
....
....

What have you learned about yourself?

....
....
....
....
....
....
....
....

What do you really (REALLY) want to achieve — the ultimate goal?

....
....
....
....
....
....
....
....
....

Why do you want it? What will give you?

....
....
....
....
....
....
....
....
....

What is your definition of success?

....
....
....
....
....
....
....
....
....

What does success look like to you? Describe the look and feel of success.

....
....
....
....
....
....
....
....
....
....

What price, if any, are you willing to pay to achieve your definition of success?

....
....
....
....
....
....
....
....
....
....
....
....
....
....

What are the barriers you have faced/are facing to achieve your goal and how are you going to tackle them now?

....
....
....
....
....
....
....
....
....
....
....
....
....
....
....

To what extent do you think your current personal brand (and the consequent impression of you people have) was a barrier to achieve "success"? Better still, how aligned is your current personal brand with your idea of "success" (I'm assuming there is some kind of disconnect between the two or you wouldn't have picked up this book in the first place)?

....
....
....
....
....
....
....
....
....
....
....
....
....
....

Write down key learning points from reviewing Jackie Kennedy and Diana, Princess of Wales style and communication through their appearance/clothes , etc.

....
....
....
....
....
....
....
....
....
....

Write down key learning points from looking at the style of other successful women and their style through key times in their career.

....
....
....
....
....
....
....
....
....
....
....
....
....
....
....
....
....
....
....
....
....
....
....
....
....
....
....
....
....

Great job.

3 things to be thankful for

Think back at the topic covered today — what are the 3 things you are grateful for, despite everything? Remember, if you can't think of any — you are not looking hard enough. Think again.

....

....

....

....

....

....

....

....

....

....

....

....

....

....

....

....

....

....

....

....

....

....

....

....

....

....

....

....

DAY 56: THINK OUTSIDE THE BOX: WHAT BOX? LOOK THE PART

*The Monkey Mind/dump the c*** exercise*

P rompt:
   Personal brand

....
....
....
....
....
....
....
....
....
....
....
....
....
....

Brand You: identifying what makes you different

To live well, get what you want, whilst being satisfied along the way, you need to know how to present and sell yourself — emphasize your qualities, gloss over the not so good sides.

We have gone through this concept but I will go over it again, with a new analogy this time: between two windows with the same objects, one well done, the other without inventiveness, we stop decisively in front of the first.

A well-defined, memorable brand is essential:

- To help customers (bosses/clients etc.) remember the product (YOU)
- To convey a simple message quickly
- To help customers distinguishing the product (YOU) from similar products (other people)
- To create a positive appeal to entice someone to buy the product (offer you a position/promotion/funding).

The good news is you can help people to see you exactly as you would like them to with a well-defined personal brand.

"You Personal Style (Brand) melds your lifestyle, finances, and identity into an overall fashion statement that makes you feel good about yourself and tells the world how to feel about you …
Getting the looks part out of the way allows you to get down to business and the true priorities of your life,"
- Suzy Gershman.

A personal brand will help you in standing out in a crowded arena and get noticed, whilst targeting your ideal customers (e.g., company / bosses / investors , etc.). Truth be said, you already have a personal brand (people's perception of you) and so far — as we have ascertained — this has not served you as well as it could have. Time to change it.

Action point

Let's work together in creating/evolving your personal brand.

First thing: making a list of adjectives that describe you physically, person-ality wise and other characteristics. Write down as many as you can think of in each column (I wrote some examples for you to start you off); they can be both positive AND negative.

Take your time and be specific.

Physical appearance	Personality traits	Additional
Example: brunette	*adventurous*	*Irish.*

Now that you have a full list it's time to do some "market research" e.g. find out how other people would describe you.

I would pick a mix of friends, family, co-workers (men and women). Ask them to be open and honest and do assure them that you would not take offense (please don't — remember they are already describing you THAT way when people ask them about you — you might as well know it).

Same drill as you did yourself:

Physical appearance	Personality traits	Additional
Example: brunette	*adventurous*	*Irish.*

This exercise will be very useful for tomorrow — good job!

3 things to be thankful for

Think back at the topic covered today — what are the 3 things you are grateful for, despite everything? Remember, if you can't think of any — you are not looking hard enough. Think again.

....
....
....
....
....
....
....
....
....
....
....
....
....
....
....
....
....
....
....
....
....
....
....
....
....
....
....

DAY 57: THINK OUTSIDE THE BOX: WHAT BOX? LOOK THE PART

The Monkey Mind/dump the c*** exercise

P **rompt:**
  Self-analysis

....
....
....
....
....
....
....
....
....
....
....
....
....

Creating your new personal brand

Presentation and selling are arts: there is definitely a dose of talent but also some professionalism that can be learned.

To present and sell yourself better, you need to know yourself well. That is, to evaluate the quality or the essential qualities on which to build a kingdom.

Needless to say personality wins, that mix of pleasant or unpleasant qualities that make an individual a person. Give yourself a sign that distinguishes you.

It must not be an "a solo" but a symphony in which a solo instrument plays the base. The same quality played on all the times is overwhelming, it wows when pulled out at the right moment.

Bluff very little and love yourself very much: don't invent "from scratch" features that you are far from possessing.

The right comparison is with actors. Each actor looks for his/her genre, then with time and experience, maybe he/she changes or integrates it. Or get good enough to recite any text as long as he/she cares.

However, when you decide what you want to bet on, get used to thinking of yourself as a person of that type. In short, enter the part until it is spontaneous and natural.

Beware of the most common mistakes:

- Haste - makes you lose sight of the goal
- Excess - never be too much. To be respected (and admired) you have to give yourself a human image, with small shadow areas that highlight and brighten qualities

- Sectorialization - once you get into character, don't abandon it. You are not bluffing; you are just working on your personality. It makes no sense to have a public and a private image. Your project is and must be a <u>total immersion</u> project.

For this project (your new brand/personal style), it is essential to choose a field of action, a field of intervention and what I mean by this, is to identify clearly what you want to achieve (what is the position, in what sector/company, what level, what success looks like) because this is the starting point (hence all the exercises we have gone through in the past days).

Action point

In yesterday's exercises you compiled a list of different adjectives/words that you think describe your persona and also you should have asked other people to do the same. Now it is time to review all the data gathered — are there any commonalities? Any surprises?

....
....
....
....
....
....
....
....
....
....
....
....

*Select just three words/phrases from the overall data that make you **different**: a unique set of three positive attributes that together create an **interesting & attractive** personal brand.*

The criteria:

1. *The brand must ring true to who you are, both from your perspective but also as others see you*
2. *The brand has a wide appeal (don't niche down too much)*
3. *The brand is easy to remember and unique*
4. *The brand positions you for the role/company at the level you are aiming at.*

The selection of the three attributes, when combined, will make you stand out positively.

....
....
....
....

How the three attributes/words are combined will be the key to a standout personal brand, starting with "looking the part".

*Let's start with looking back at your mood board, your images of what success "looks like," examples of how Jackie Kennedy/Diana, Princess of Wales and the other successful women you admire communicate through their personal style. Select amongst all the images/examples the most aligned and representative of your **new** chosen brand (add more images if you need to) and create the New YOU mood board.*

. . .

This page is left intentionally blank so you can stick all your pictures there, ready for the next two days - I know, I know, normally the weekend is for rest and relaxation, not this one. I want to make sure that, by the end of the workbook, you are ready to "Look The Part".

3 things to be thankful for

Think back at the topic covered today — what are the 3 things you are grateful for, despite everything? Remember, if you can't think of any — you are not looking hard enough. Think again.

....
....
....
....
....
....
....
....
....
....
....
....
....
....
....
....
....
....
....
....
....
....
....
....
....
....

DAY 58: NO REST FOR THE WICKED - WARDROBE CLEAN OUT

The Monkey Mind/dump the c*** exercise

P rompt:

Clothes and hoarding

....
....
....
....
....
....
....
....
....
....
....
....
....

The purpose of this weekend is to review your current wardrobe: get rid of excess and inappropriate clothing (for your new brand) and design a small, basic wardrobe that will look attractive and appropriate for all your lifestyle/business activities whilst being totally aligned with your new personal style/brand.

Remember the analogy with actors: once into character...

It makes no sense to have a public and a private image. Your project is and must be a <u>total immersion</u> project.

Ready to rock?

Action point

To start with, I'd suggest wearing good underwear (bear with me) and something comfy that it is easy to take off and on. Then gather some rubbish/recycling bags and cleaning materials (again, bear with me …).

Now, empty your wardrobe/s and drawers — completely — and start cleaning (let's face it, when was the last time you deep cleaned them?).

Yup, that's right — when you finish today you want a clean and fresh space for the "New YOU" clothes to be in.

Ok, go....

....

....

....

....

....

....

....

Cleaning done?

. . .

Now, look carefully at the pile of clothes on your bed/floor, wherever you put them ...

Look at them mercilessly, e.g., if they look tatty, raggedy it is time to take them to their rightful resting place, the clothes cemetery a.k.a. the recycling bin (not to charity).

Go on, this is where one of those recycling bags will come handy ...

....
....
....
....
....
....
....
....
....
....
....
....
....
....
....
....
....

Done? I shall refrain from asking how many bags, your secret is safe ;-)

And now the fun begins.

. . .

*Let's pretend you are out shopping somewhere really fancy, get yourself a nice glass of wine (or a cup of tea if you prefer) and now you are going to try on **E-V-E-R-Y-T-H-I-N-G** they/you have in the shop, a.k.a. your clothes on the floor.*

Be honest, objective and look not only how they sit on you but also how they make you feel: sexy? Powerful? Young? Frumpy?

As you are trying them on, divide the clothes in three piles:

1. *Fit just right*
2. *Too big*
3. *Too small.*

....
....
....
....
....
....
....
....
....
....
....
....
....
....
....
....

Done? Time for a quick comfort break ;-)

· · ·

*Now that you are back, you can put the clothes from **Pile 1** (fit just right) back in the cleaned wardrobe that should be fully dry and smelling awesome by now. We will look at them again tomorrow.*

__Pile 3__ (clothes too small — a.k.a. hanging on to the "dream"): if you were like the majority of women, including me, you'd probably have a collection (small or vast) of different sizes there.

No judging, we have all done it. Now though is the time to be realistic.
Ask yourself a very simple question: am I committed to lose all the weight that I need in order to be able to fit into this size/these sizes again?

Only you know the answer to that question — my advice here would be to ditch anything smaller than one or two sizes at most (let's face it, if you were that way inclined and you really had wanted to, you would have by now).

Ok then, the discarded clothes are going into another recycling bag, ready for their new home: the charity shop. Leave the remaining clothes, if any, on one side for now.

__Pile 2__ (clothes too big — a.k.a. the "just in case I put on weight again"): firstly, THIS has got to STOP! Not even going to attempt at being nice here …

Secondly, these clothes could be boosting your existing wardrobe right now, with just a few modifications. But for now, you are going to put them neatly on a chair, ready for tomorrow, creating your capsule wardrobe for the "New YOU".

That's it for today; you deserve a medal (or a bottle of wine).

3 things to be thankful for

Think back at the topic covered today — what are the 3 things you are grateful for, despite everything? Remember, if you can't think of any — you are not looking hard enough. Think again.

....
....
....
....
....
....
....
....
....
....
....
....
....
....
....
....
....
....
....
....
....
....
....
....
....
....
....

DAY 59: NO REST OR RELAXATION - PUTTING IT ALL TOGETHER

The Monkey Mind/dump the c*** exercise

P**rompt:**
    *Imagine that you have achieved the success you want, you have arrived at the position/role , etc., that you want and imagine being interviewed by a magazine for an article: they want to know everything about you — your routine, your exercise program, your home decor, the music you listen to, the books you read and ALL about your **amazing look**. E-V-E-R-Y-T-H-I-N-G.*

....
....
....
....
....
....
....
....
....
....
....

Hello again! Yesterday we got rid of excess and inappropriate clothing (the raggedy and too small ones) and today we are going to design a small, basic wardrobe that will look attractive and appropriate for all your lifestyle/business activities and aligned with your new brand/personal style.

Action point

Let's start with the "wearing good underwear and something comfy that it is easy to take off and on" thingy again.

Then, let's revisit day 57:

- *The three chosen attributes/words that sum up your brand*
- *Your new mood board with the selection of images aligned and representative of your new chosen brand and all the examples from Jackie Kennedy/Diana, Princess of Wales and the other successful women you admire and how they communicate through their personal style.*

And now, look at your remaining clothes:

__Pile 1__ - the "fit just right" clothes hanging neatly in the wardrobe
__Pile 2__ - the "too big" clothes piled on a chair
__Pile 3__ - the one-size "too small" clothes remaining.

Are your clothes (Pile 1, 2 & 3) representative of your new persona and your (career/lifestyle) aspirations? If not right now, could they (by mixing them up, adding accessories , etc.)?

Take some time and mix and match, combine your clothes to produce different looks aligned to your mood board.

. . .

Write up/assemble as many outfits as you can to cover both your professional and leisure time, as minimum at least five different outfits. The more you can use single pieces of clothing to make up different looks the better.

....
....
....
....
....
....
....
....
....
....
....
....
....
....
....
....
....
....
....
....
....
....
....
....
....
....

You may find that you now have a few items of clothing (from one or all piles) that you have not used at all. Put them away neatly.

You can revisit them in a few weeks and, if you cannot find any use within your new personal style, you can then donate them to charity.

• • •

You may have also noticed that you are missing a few key pieces — clothes or accessories: this is your <u>shopping list.</u>

*On the other hand, you should also have quite a few options/looks that represent the "New YOU" from one or all piles; the clothes you've used from **Pile 2**, the too big ones, you can now definitely take to amend/alter so they fit you better as you know you'll need them.*

*The clothes you've used from **Pile 3**, the one size too small ones, you can take out regularly or keep them in a place where you can see them easily — an incentive to lose those last few pounds/dress size.*

To ensure though that your new personal brand/style becomes second nature, you will need to design and organize your closet in a simple manner, with practical use in mind.

There are different ways to arrange clothes and accessories:

- *By category*
- *By color group*
- *By outfit.*

The important thing is to use a system that works for you, is easy to follow and doesn't require too much thinking (especially at the beginning when you are still road-testing your new brand).

Now select your system and organize your entire wardrobe accordingly (category — color group — outfit).

....
....
....
....
....
....
....
....
....
....
....
....
....
....
....
....
....
....
....

You should now have:

- A freshly clean closet and drawers
- A small (or big depending how many clothes you had to start with) wardrobe that is fully aligned with your new/upgraded personal style/brand that can take you seamlessly from work to leisure with ease.

Great job!

3 things to be thankful for

Think back at the topic covered today — what are the 3 things you are grateful for, despite everything? Remember, if you can't think of any — you are not looking hard enough. Think again.

....
....
....
....
....
....
....
....
....
....
....
....
....
....
....
....
....
....
....
....
....
....
....
....
....
....

DAY 60: LAUNCHING AND PROMOTING YOUR NEW BRAND

The Monkey Mind/dump the c*** exercise

P **rompt:**
    Future

....
....
....
....
....
....
....
....
....
....
....
....
....
....

Launching and promoting your new brand

Now that you've developed your brand, what do you do with it?

Well, now that you have created a personal brand, you need to advertise it. Everyone needs to know about it — it doesn't do any good if it is just in your mind or stays in this workbook.

What you need to do is to communicate what makes you different and helping people frame you in their mind. It is easy: after all they can only evaluate what you show them and it is possible to take control over situations by being consistent and conscious of the messages you send.

And the more you tell people about your new label/brand, the easier it will become.

Two important lessons taken from Marketing 101:

1. Brand consistency is absolute key — same as in advertising, your brand image must remain the same every time the consumer (your boss, prospective boss, investors, family etc.) is exposed to it
2. Brand recall — this essentially measure of how easily people remember what the brand stands for (the three attributes/words). This is crucial to establish the brand.

Consistency is the easier one to achieve:

from now on, everything that you do, wear, say and write about yourself should be consistent with your new/revamped personal style/brand.

. . .

And this means everything that you do, wear, say and write about yourself with your family, friends, your Nan, your dates etc.etc. including a complete review of <u>ALL</u> your social media profiles (yes, that's right): LinkedIn, Instagram, Facebook, Pinterest and any other you might have.

Remember: you are an actor fully immersing yourself in your character, your best self.

Brand recall will be highly dependent on both actively advertising your new brand and the consistency in which you are applying it (after all, you can't say one thing and do another).

Think about a product re-launch: you are about to embark into a massive "New YOU" advertising drive to reach new markets and customers (your new company/position) and upgrade/reposition the views your current customers and markets have of you.

Whether consciously or not, you advertise yourself constantly.

This time it will be a conscious effort, starting with a slow transition with the nearest and dearest, a.k.a. your family and friends. I'm assuming here that you are not likely to be able to "disappear" and not see them for a prolonged period of time. Plus they've known you all their and your life so you'll need to work a bit longer and skillfully to shift their perceptions.

The idea is to project your new/upgraded brand (the three chosen positive attributes together with the associated look) to them in a subtle way.

The NeuroLinguistic Programming technique of Mirroring and Matching can be very useful to reinforce and shift your message.

Mirroring is one of the most useful NLP techniques there are, is innate and even chimps use mirroring within their groups.

Pay attention whether people are visual, audial, or kinaesthetic (you do so by listening to their language patterns) and consequently adapt your communication/language style to suit the specific audience and have more impact.

State	Primary sense	Language patterns
Visual	Sight	I see; it looks good
Audial	Hearing	Sounds good; that rings a bell
Kinaesthetic	Feeling	That doesn't feel right; I can't put my finger on it

How?

Start by selecting a few people that have the widest impact amongst your family and friends (the more mouthy and opinionated, once they get it, they will help "spreading the message" and your new brand).

Allow yourself a few weeks to embed the message and make each interaction count: beside wearing your "new clothes," drop hints during casual conversation introducing your three main brand attributes.

As you interact with them, remember to use "right" language for your audience in line with their primary state and sense (I see, I hear, I feel).

To introduce your new brand in your current workplace/work environment, you have a couple of options:

1. Straight after the weekend spent re-arranging your wardrobe (or a weekend); or
2. A "big reveal" e.g. after an holiday.

If you choose option 1, you can use the same tactics used with your family and friends: pick 5 people (the ones with the most influence and wider net, must include your boss) and make a conscious effort to reinforce your brand in each and every interaction.

If you choose option 2, "The big reveal," I'd suggest firstly preparing the so-called "30-second commercial", a ready-made pitch to sell your new brand. Make it short, make it snappy and ensure you use the three attributes of your brand in a catchy phrase describing your metamorphosis. This way when people ask you about your new look, you'll have something ready that you have practiced and positions the way you want.

People should be able to remember your brand easily, be able to describe you "the right way" and repeat this accurately to others.

You'll know this is working when:

- People look like they positively recognize your description/attributes when you talk about it
- People start describing you that way to others
- People start inviting you to events, talk to you about projects , etc., aligned with your new brand (after all the purpose of all this is to get you your next coveted position).

Ok then, now it's the time to make some decisions and plan the way forward.

. . .

Action point

Look back at the three main attributes/words that describe your "new" brand and the Monkey Mind/dump the c*** media profile of the new you.

Review it, refine it and make sure you re-iterate the three attributes/words throughout the piece.

....
....
....
....
....
....
....
....
....
....
....

Now, crystalize and summarize your media profile into a short and sweet 30-second commercial for the New You.

....
....
....
....
....
....
....
....
....
....
....
....
....
....

Mirror and Match practice = identify five key people amongst your family and friends that you can start to Mirror and Match (be careful not to come across as parroting) and talk about your new brand attributes/showcase your new brand. It would be useful to start with people that have the same language patterns you have (e.g., Visual/Audial/Kinaesthetic) — this will make it much easier. Plan how you will approach the subject/introduce your new brand attributes and schedule over the course of the next few weeks.

....
....
....
....
....
....
....
....
....
....
....
....

Repeat the exercise for people with different language patterns from yours. Plan and schedule.

....
....
....
....
....
....
....
....
....
....
....
....

Mirror and Match practice = identify now the five people at work that you are going to carry out the same practice with. As before, plan how you will approach the subject/introduce your new brand attributes and schedule over the course of the next few weeks.

....
....
....
....
....
....
....
....
....
....
....
....

Irrespectively if you are opting for a "big reveal" or not in your current workplace/work environment, you'll need it anyway for new opportunities outside your work circle. Planning would be good here (hint, hint)....

....
....
....
....
....
....
....
....
....
....
....
....

3 things to be thankful for

Think back at the topic covered today — what are the 3 things you are grateful for, despite everything? Remember, if you can't think of any — you are not looking hard enough. Think again.

....
....
....
....
....
....
....
....
....
....
....
....
....
....
....
....
....
....
....
....
....
....
....
....
....
....

ACT THE PART

30 DAYS TO REBOOT YOUR LIFE

DAY 61: THERE IS NOTHING TO FEAR BUT FEAR ITSELF

The Monkey Mind/dump the c*** exercise

P**rompt:**
    What comes to mind when thinking of the words taking action?

....
....
....
....
....
....
....
....
....
....
....
....
....
....
....
....

The fear process

Oh yes, it is the fear process again. It is one of the most powerful and useful I have ever encountered; I do it and re-do it again, and so should you.

Fear contributes to self-sabotage; it keeps us from extending ourselves and taking chances. Fear keeps us from taking action. And let's face it: if you want to really reboot your career, just putting a strategy together and rebooting your image is not going to help you on its own. You need to take action. If you haven't so far, then you have some type of fear in there, somewhere.

"Fear is the mind-killer" - Frank Herbert.

Ready?

Ok, ready or not, here it is — just do it, will you?.

A quick reminder on how the process works:

A fear I have about .... is that ....

1 If you don't think you have fears about taking action to achieve your career goal, you are definitely lying to yourself.

2 Whatever comes up, do not judge and do not try to deduce what it means and if it applies to you. Write it down.

3 If a thought arises that is so upsetting that you are uncomfortable writing it down, write it down anyway!

4 Don't edit your thoughts. And don't waste any time trying to justify

them. Don't get entangled with thinking that writing your fears down will make them real, either. The purpose of this process is to let go of your fears, and you can do so by discharging them from your mind onto the page.

Write as fast as possible, following the process. Write down at least a full page. MINIMUM.

Before you start, think about what brought you here, your professional situation and what you are trying to achieve.

BREATHE.

Breathe again.

Turn the page and start the process.

Go ahead.

A fear I have about taking action is that

....
....
....
....
....
....
....
....
....
....
....
....
....
....
....
....
....
....
....
....
....
....
....
....
....
....
....
....
....

Take a moment to write down more things that fear has kept you from doing throughout your career and life — things that you really wanted to do.

....

....

....

....

....

....

....

....

....

....

....

....

....

....

....

....

....

....

....

....

....

....

....

....

....

....

....

....

....

....

Done?

And now, to move on from here write the following:

"I am willing to act in the presence of fear. I hereby resolve for the next 30 days to commit and persist in this journey and that I will not allow fear to keep me from doing something I genuinely desire to do".

Then sign your name and date it.

Name ....

Date ....

Enough for today — good job!

3 things to be thankful for

Think back at the topic covered today — what are the 3 things you are grateful for, despite everything? Remember, if you can't think of any — you are not looking hard enough. Think again.

....

....

....

....

....

....

....

....

....

....

....

....

....

....

....

....

....

....

....

....

....

....

....

....

....

....

You see? It wasn't that difficult, was it? Great work.

DAY 62: WHERE ARE YOU NOW?

The Monkey Mind/dump the c*** exercise

Prompt:
   What comes to mind when thinking of taking action to increase diversity in leadership?

....

....

....

....

....

....

....

....

....

....

....

....

....

The Overview

Research from many worldwide organizations has found that three women or more are needed to create a "critical mass," leading to better financial performance, yet only 20.1% have at least three women. And yes, I'm repeating myself, but it is important to remember.

MSCI found that having three or more women changes the boardroom dynamics and "enhances the likelihood that women's voices and ideas are heard, " resulting in better financial results.

They also found that companies with fewer women on boards had more governance-related controversies than average.

It is not just about equality and all things nice, women on board affect key indicators, including financials. If that is not important to remember I don't know what is.

Action Point

So far you researched and raised your awareness on diversity, gathered information about your customers, markets, demographics and compared the male to female ratio of your sector/customer base to the company you work for.

You have also ascertained the number of females in middle management and leadership positions compared to males in the same position.

Additionally you have looked at how leadership (both male and female) is representative of your customer base and the company brand image. Finally you looked at some suggestions on how to improve.

. . .

Now, the important stuff. Does your company have a diversity and inclusion strategy and plan?

....
....
....
....

Have the been widely communicated across the company?

....
....
....
....
....

What have been the key actions?

....
....
....
....
....

What have been the key results?

....
....
....
....
....

What didn't work so well and why?

....
....
....
....
....
....
....
....
....
....

What would you have done differently and why?

....
....
....
....
....
....
....
....
....
....

Is diversity and inclusion one of the company target which is tracked and bonusable? E.g. is it part and parcel of managers's objectives?

....
....
....
....
....

The UN Women "Roadmap for Substantive Equality: 2030" aims to repeal and amend discriminatory laws against women whilst ensuring that regulations are supportive in general of gender equality & women's human rights.

Most importantly, it focuses not only on achieving legislative reform but equally that they are put into practice.

Gender-discriminatory laws are often rooted in discriminatory social norms, which remain pervasive and are difficult to change.

Taking action is what matters.

Action Point

List actions you have taken professionally to change social norms you believed to be discriminatory.

....
....
....
....
....
....
....
....
....
....
....

Great job!

3 things to be thankful for

Think back at the topic covered today — what are the 3 things you are grateful for, despite everything? Remember, if you can't think of any — you are not looking hard enough. Think again.

....
....
....
....
....
....
....
....
....
....
....
....
....
....
....
....
....
....
....
....
....
....
....
....
....
....

DAY 63: ONCE UPON A TIME

The Monkey Mind/dump the c*** exercise

P**rompt:**
What is a woman's place today?

....
....
....
....
....
....
....
....
....
....
....
....
....
....

A woman's place

We have seen previously what a "woman's place" is or seen to be has varied throughout history from warriors, powerful priestesses, and political leaders to portrayals inferior to men. Looking at the position of women at different points in history can show us how our society has grown and changed and help us understand the present, including barriers.

Women have gained and lost power at different times in history; they have been painted and portrayed beautifully whilst not affecting their lives on a day-to-day basis, aka a woman's place was the homemaker.

The most significant gains inequality had to wait until the twentieth century, for example, with the Suffragettes' successful campaign for women being granted the right to vote. World War I and two also showed that women could contribute to the economy and work both inside and outside the home, taking men's places in factories.

The sixties and seventies and the advent of feminism further changed some of society's perceptions and, most importantly, changed women's own beliefs.

Action point

You have previously looked back in history and a woman's place in those times and how women were expected to look like.

What specific actions moved the needle further each time?

....
....
....
....
....
....

What beliefs changed to move the needle further women?

....
....
....
....
....

What did you learn from the three heroines you chose?

....
....
....
....
....

What specific actions did they take?

....
....
....
....
....

Shorter day today, good job.

3 things to be thankful for

Think back at the topic covered today — what are the 3 things you are grateful for, despite everything? Remember, if you can't think of any — you are not looking hard enough. Think again.

....
....
....
....
....
....
....
....
....
....
....
....
....
....
....
....
....
....
....
....
....
....
....
....
....
....
....

DAY 64: WHAT ARE YOUR BARRIERS - PART 1

The Monkey Mind/dump the c*** exercise

Prompt:
   What comes to mind when you hear the word barrier? (Yes, again).

....
....
....
....
....
....
....
....
....
....
....
....
....
....

Cultural, religious & family paradigms

I am going to say it again: religion is a controversial topic. It is difficult to talk about it without insulting/annoying someone somewhere and without being disputed on the interpretation/misinterpretation of the scripture/s. I do not wish to offend anyone or to challenge your beliefs.

I just want to consciously raise your awareness that religion has played/is playing and will continue to play a big part in the way different groups of people perceive themselves. It plays a very big part in your definition of "what good looks like," including women and their role in society and that there is a correlation between the two.

Many religions share the same characterizations and expectations of a traditional female role, gender and sexual identity, and unique image expectations that determine what you believe you can and cannot do, how you should do it, and why and how you should look and why.

Action Point

What actions have you avoided specifically because of your cultural background, religion, and family paradigms? How have these non-actions limited you — if they did, that is.

....
....
....
....
....
....
....
....
....

For women who wish to have children, there are additional expectations.

Society is made of tribal congregations (religious and secular institutions, communities and families) all with their individual, sometimes divergent and sometimes mutually supportive views of a "woman's place," a "mother's duty" and "the right way of doing things".

Action Point

What are your inherited views about motherhood and a "mother's duty" and how have they affected your professional decisions?

....
....
....
....
....
....
....
....
....
....

Are these views supportive or conflicting with your desire for professional success and climbing the ladder? How much (or little) have they limited your ambition?

....
....
....
....
....
....
....
....
....

Gosh, that was heavy - You need a break for today.

3 things to be thankful for

Think back at the topic covered today — what are the 3 things you are grateful for, despite everything? Remember, if you can't think of any — you are not looking hard enough. Think again.

....
....
....
....
....
....
....
....
....
....
....
....
....
....
....
....
....
....
....
....
....
....
....
....
....
....

DAY 65: WHAT ARE YOUR BARRIERS - PART 2

*The Monkey Mind/dump the c*** exercise*

Prompt:
    What comes to mind when you hear the words "good girl"? How does she act?

....
....
....
....
....
....
....
....
....
....
....
....
....
....

The "good girl syndrome"

Although there is definitely the outer game of society/family paradigms and so on, there is also a far more important inner game, your own perceptions, your own decisions, belief systems that drive behavior and choices made — the "good girl syndrome".

Rachida Dati comes to mind, the French Justice Minister under French President Nicolas Sarkozy who went back to work five days after having her first child by Caesarean section. Seeing her going back as what is perceived (by whom?) too soon started a barrage and ping-pong of comments and articles, some quite bitching and derogative and some alleging bullying from Sarkozy (and the worse ones were from women).

Better still, people were discussing if she is *"right to put the demands of her career ahead of her child? Or is she crazy to miss out on some of the most precious months of her life? "* like there is only one way of being a mother AND a career woman at the same time.

Action Point
How much have your cultural/religious and family paradigms conditioned your behavior, personally and professionally, as a woman? Go deep, take your time here.

....
....
....
....
....
....
....
....
....

....
....
....
....
....
....
....
....
....
....
....
....
....
....
....
....
....
....
....
....
....
....

Short day today — great job.

3 things to be thankful for

Think back at the topic covered today — what are the 3 things you are grateful for, despite everything? Remember, if you can't think of any — you are not looking hard enough. Think again.

....

....

....

....

....

....

....

....

....

....

....

....

....

....

....

....

....

....

....

....

....

....

....

....

....

....

DAY 66: WHAT ARE YOUR BARRIERS - PART 3

*The Monkey Mind/dump the c*** exercise*

P**rompt:**
   What comes to mind when you hear the words age "bias"?

....

....

....

....

....

....

....

....

....

....

....

....

....

....

Who's a "good girl"?

Today we are going to delve even deeper, if possible, into "your" idea of how a "good girl" acts.

Action point

You should now have a good idea of your beliefs derived from the social/religious and family paradigms regarding the "good girl" syndrome and how it affects career choices, image , etc.

Now think back at times when you applied this "learnt judgement" and passed it onto others: go as far back or as near as you need to. I invite you again to do so on purpose and see how and if your behavior changed with time.

Describe three different occasions at three different times in your life when you have demonstrated bias towards other women, actions they took not conforming with your learnt "good girl" syndrome belief (it is hard to admit, but we all do it and we all project our beliefs with our behavior — the point here is to have awareness).

....
....
....
....
....
....
....
....
....
....
....
....
....
....

How would you/could behave differently now, if the same situations arise again?

....
....
....
....
....
....
....
....
....
....
....
....
....
....
....
....
....
....
....
....
....
....
....
....

With understanding and acknowledging your own biases, you are taking step forward to a more level playing field — for yourself and other women. Congratulations.

3 *things to be thankful for*

Think back at the topic covered today — what are the 3 things you are grateful for, despite everything? Remember, if you can't think of any — you are not looking hard enough. Think again.

....
....
....
....
....
....
....
....
....
....
....
....
....
....
....
....
....
....
....
....
....
....
....
....
....
....
....

DAY 67: REST, RELAXATION AND SOME REFLECTION

The Monkey Mind/dump the c*** exercise

P **rompt:**
   Self-confidence

....
....
....
....
....
....
....
....
....
....
....
....
....
....

This page is intentionally left blank

3 things to be thankful for

Think back at the topic covered today — what are the 3 things you are grateful for, despite everything? Remember, if you can't think of any — you are not looking hard enough. Think again.

....

....

....

....

....

....

....

....

....

....

....

....

....

....

....

....

....

....

....

....

....

....

....

....

....

DAY 68: REST, RELAXATION AND SOME REFLECTION

The Monkey Mind/dump the c*** exercise

P **rompt:**
   Time for action

....
....
....
....
....
....
....
....
....
....
....
....
....
....
....

This page is intentionally left blank

3 things to be thankful for

Think back at the topic covered today — what are the 3 things you are grateful for, despite everything? Remember, if you can't think of any — you are not looking hard enough. Think again.

....
....
....
....
....
....
....
....
....
....
....
....
....
....
....
....
....
....
....
....
....
....
....
....
....

DAY 69: SUCCESS IS A RELATIVE THING - PART 1

The Monkey Mind/dump the c*** exercise

Prompt:
> *What comes to mind when you hear the word SUCCESSFUL in life?*

....
....
....
....
....
....
....
....
....
....
....
....
....
....

What does success mean to you overall?

Success means so many things to so many people; if you don't define what good (or great) looks like, you will be always chasing something, the next shiny object, unachievable targets and never be quite satisfied.

Action Point

Pause for a minute and think — jot down what is your definition of a successful life — include both relationships, family, lifestyle AND career.

....
....
....
....
....
....
....
....

Where does this definition originate from (family, friends, peers)?

....
....
....
....
....
....
....
....

Is this definition still relevant to you now? If yes (or no), why yes (or no)?

....
....
....
....
....
....
....

Has this definition changed in the last few years? If yes, what has changed?

....
....
....
....
....
....
....

What has been the constant (as compared to the variable) in your definition of success?

....
....
....
....
....
....

Well done.

3 things to be thankful for

Think back at the topic covered today — what are the 3 things you are grateful for, despite everything? Remember, if you can't think of any — you are not looking hard enough. Think again.

....

....

....

....

....

....

....

....

....

....

....

....

....

....

....

....

....

....

....

....

....

....

....

....

....

....

DAY 70: SUCCESS IS A RELATIVE THING - PART 2

The Monkey Mind/dump the c*** exercise

P**rompt:**
   What do you feel when you hear the words YOU CAN'T?

....
....
....
....
....
....
....
....
....
....
....
....
....
....
....

What does success really really really mean to you?

Success means so many things to so many people; we have looked at what is your definition of success and how that has changed from a rational viewpoint. Now is the time to go deeper into your feelings. NO, DEEPER. DEEPER.

Action point

Take some time to think about what success really means to you: a job well done? Position? Power? Most importantly what are the actions required to achieve it?

....
....
....
....
....
....
....
....
....
....
....

What has truly stopped you so far? Think of internal barrier here.

....
....
....
....
....
....
....

What else has stopped you? Now you can think of external barriers.

....
....
....
....
....

What actions should you have taken to achieve your idea of success? Why didn't you?

....
....
....
....
....
....
....
....
....
....
....
....
....
....

What is the destination and why? Is this still the same one or has it changed? If so, why and how?

....
....
....
....
....

What will make you feel truly successful right now?

....

....

....

....

....

....

How can you start feeling that now? Once you understand what success means to you, you can then recognize it and celebrate it — daily. Feeling successful, fulfilled breathes confidence — the more you recognize your achievements and feel good about them — the more confident you feel and the bigger things you will attempt, get my drift? ;-)

.

....

....

....

....

....

....

....

....

....

....

....

....

....

....

....

Great job.

3 things to be thankful for

Think back at the topic covered today — what are the 3 things you are grateful for, despite everything? Remember, if you can't think of any — you are not looking hard enough. Think again.

....

....

....

....

....

....

....

....

....

....

....

....

....

....

....

....

....

....

....

....

....

....

....

....

....

....

DAY 71: WHAT IS YOUR WHY?

The Monkey Mind/dump the c*** exercise

P**rompt:**
  So, what do you really need now?

....
....
....
....
....
....
....
....
....
....
....
....
....
....

The Maslow Hierarchy of Needs

Let's revisit Maslow's Hierarchy of Needs, e.g., people are motivated to fulfill basic needs before moving on to the more advanced needs, trying to understand what makes people happy and what they do/would do to meet their needs.

The need for security and safety is a primary need, all about control and order in our lives and consequent behaviors (financial security, health and wellness, protection against accidents and injury).

The need for appreciation and respect, e.g., gaining the respect and appreciation of others, leads to the need to accomplish things and then have efforts recognized together with the feeling of accomplishment and prestige, self-esteem and personal worth.

Tony Robbins talks about the same drivers of human behaviors in a more fluid way:
- Certainty and security
- Uncertainty and variety
- Significance
- Love & Connection
- Growth
- Contribution.

Basic human needs need to be fulfilled, and human beings will do whatever is necessary to meet them, even though, logically, it is contrary to what they say they want. Including you.

Action Point

What is stopping you right now from taking action and achieving your dream career (to be clear, we are not talking here about any real or perceived external forces)? What need/s are you trying to meet?

....
....
....
....
....
....
....
....
....
....

What is "reasons" have you given yourself to justify not taking action?

....
....
....
....
....
....
....
....
....

How can you meet your need/s in a different way that doesn't hinder you?

....
....
....
....
....
....
....
....
....

You are doing great.

3 things to be thankful for

Think back at the topic covered today — what are the 3 things you are grateful for, despite everything? Remember, if you can't think of any — you are not looking hard enough. Think again.

....
....
....
....
....
....
....
....
....
....
....
....
....
....
....
....
....
....
....
....
....
....
....
....
....
....

DAY 72: WHAT IS THE PRICE?

*The Monkey Mind/dump the c*** exercise*

Prompt:
   What is your real price?

....
....
....
....
....
....
....
....
....
....
....
....
....
....

Everyone pays a price

Leadership requires 100% commitment – Everyone pays a price.

Action Point

What "price to pay" are you willing to pay for success/the ultimate position? What sacrifices are you willing to make, if any?

....
....
....
....
....
....
....
....
....
....
....
....
....
....
....
....
....
....
....
....
....
....
....
....
....
....
....
....

What is really stopping you from taking action?

....
....
....
....
....
....
....
....
....
....
....
....
....
....
....
....
....
....
....
....
....
....
....

And on that note, I'll leave you to ponder...

3 things to be thankful for

Think back at the topic covered today — what are the 3 things you are grateful for, despite everything? Remember, if you can't think of any — you are not looking hard enough. Think again.

....

....

....

....

....

....

....

....

....

....

....

....

....

....

....

....

....

....

....

....

....

....

....

....

....

....

DAY 73: PERFECTION IS BORING - BE AWESOME INSTEAD

The Monkey Mind/dump the c*** exercise

P **rompt:**
    Are you a perfectionist?

....
....
....
....
....
....
....
....
....
....
....
....
....
....

Wonder Woman does not exist

Wonder Woman does not exist. Period.
Just beautiful strong wilful women.

Silence your inner critic — do you and what works for you.

Action Point

Are you a perfectionist? How many things have postponed in your life, your career because you were waiting for the perfect moment? List them all. Go on, I'll wait …

....
....
....
....
....
....
....
....
....
....
....
....
....
....
....
....

STOP IT!!!

3 things to be thankful for

Think back at the topic covered today — what are the 3 things you are grateful for, despite everything? Remember, if you can't think of any — you are not looking hard enough. Think again.

....

....

....

....

....

....

....

....

....

....

....

....

....

....

....

....

....

....

....

....

....

....

....

....

....

DAY 74: REST, RELAXATION AND SOME REFLECTION

The Monkey Mind/dump the c*** exercise

P**rompt:**
Forgiveness and mistakes

....
....
....
....
....
....
....
....
....
....
....
....
....
....
....

This page is intentionally left blank

3 things to be thankful for

Think back at the topic covered today — what are the 3 things you are grateful for, despite everything? Remember, if you can't think of any — you are not looking hard enough. Think again.

....

....

....

....

....

....

....

....

....

....

....

....

....

....

....

....

....

....

....

....

....

....

....

....

....

DAY 75: REST, RELAXATION AND SOME REFLECTION

The Monkey Mind/dump the c*** exercise

Prompt:
    Self-discipline

....
....
....
....
....
....
....
....
....
....
....
....
....
....
....

This page is intentionally left blank

3 things to be thankful for

Think back at the topic covered today — what are the 3 things you are grateful for, despite everything? Remember, if you can't think of any — you are not looking hard enough. Think again.

....
....
....
....
....
....
....
....
....
....
....
....
....
....
....
....
....
....
....
....
....
....
....
....
....
....
....

DAY 76: THINK OUTSIDE THE BOX: WHAT BOX? ACT THE PART

The Monkey Mind/dump the c*** exercise

P **rompt:**
  Confidence

....
....
....
....
....
....
....
....
....
....
....
....
....
....

Fake it til you make it - Part 1

"Fake it till you make it" is a commonly used English saying which advocates that, by imitating confidence and/or competence a person can actually realize those qualities and achieve the results wanted.

"Fake it till you make it" does not equate to being a completely different person to what you are and/or being unauthentic.

It does instead mean, well at least for me in this context, working with some elements of your character, personality and/or skills that need practice and improving them to finally unleash your Best Self, both professionally and personally.

Remember the mind can be tricked — acting a certain way allows your brain to "rehearse" new ways until you have actually learned what you need to and turned into the real deal.

> *"If you're presenting yourself with confidence,*
> *you can pull off pretty much anything."*-
> **Katy Perry.**

Action point

Let's look back at the Fear Process exercises on Day 1, Day 31 and Day 61: how many different types of fear did you list? Was there a pattern by any chance? Describe the pattern/common thread.

....
....
....
....
....
....
....
....
....
....
....
....
....

Let's quickly recap on some of the things that fear(s) has kept you from doing throughout your life — things that you really wanted to do.

....
....
....
....
....
....
....
....
....
....
....
....

OK, let's dig a bit deeper now: can you identify the root causes for the fear/s? What are they? Again, is there a common denominator? What is it?

....
....
....
....
....
....
....
....
....
....
....
....
....

Write it down. List the specific aspects that you'd like to work on (for example confidence or self belief , etc., you get my gist here ...).

....
....
....
....
....
....
....
....
....
....
....
....

Good job, well done.

3 things to be thankful for

Think back at the topic covered today — what are the 3 things you are grateful for, despite everything? Remember, if you can't think of any — you are not looking hard enough. Think again.

....
....
....
....
....
....
....
....
....
....
....
....
....
....
....
....
....
....
....
....
....
....
....
....
....
....

DAY 77: THINK OUTSIDE THE BOX:
WHAT BOX? ACT THE PART

The Monkey Mind/dump the c*** exercise

P rompt:
Behavior

....
....
....
....
....
....
....
....
....
....
....
....
....
....

Fake it till you make it - Part 2

"Fake it till you make it" advocates that, by imitating confidence and/or competence, a person can actually realize those qualities and achieve the results wanted.

Today let's follow on from yesterday's exercises and build on those, identifying three characteristics that you currently do not possess that are however necessary for you to achieve the next step in your career ladder.

I'd suggest looking at characteristics that are adjacent and complimentary to what comes natural to you to start with.

I follow the Tim Ferriss way of thinking — it is better to focus on your strengths than your weakness — this is because in working on your strengths it is easier and quicker to maximize the improvements and achieve greatness while working.

I know we are trying to "fake it..." here but baby steps here, baby steps...

Action point

What are your main strengths and talents (things you do extremely well with minimum effort, easily and enjoy)?

....
....
....
....
....
....
....
....
....

What are the characteristics that you currently do not possess but necessary for your next position/s which are adjacent to your main strengths and talents (A.K.A. something that stretches you a little without pushing off a cliff so to speak)?

....
....
....
....
....
....
....
....
....
....
....
....
....

Now think about how you could leverage your top strengths and talents to act out what you need to learn instead (yes, I know, you need to do some work here and think. It isn't called a workbook for nothing).

....
....
....
....
....
....
....
....
....
....
....
....
....

Next, what can you start doing right now to work on the characteristics that serve you the most (for the purpose of climbing the career ladder)?

....

....

....

....

....

....

....

....

....

....

....

....

....

....

....

....

....

....

....

....

....

....

....

....

....

....

....

....

....

....

....

....

....

....

....

3 things to be thankful for

Think back at the topic covered today — what are the 3 things you are grateful for, despite everything? Remember, if you can't think of any — you are not looking hard enough. Think again.

....

....

....

....

....

....

....

....

....

....

....

....

....

....

....

....

....

....

....

....

....

....

....

....

....

DAY 78: THINK OUTSIDE THE BOX: WHAT BOX? ACT THE PART

The Monkey Mind/dump the c*** exercise

P rompt:
Mentor

....
....
....
....
....
....
....
....
....
....
....
....
....
....

If you want to be the best, you need to learn from the best – I have not invented this phrase — you can hear it for the lips of the most successful entrepreneurs, CEOs, billionaires out there. And that is the point.

You need someone who has been there, seen it, done it and got the t-shirt so to speak and you can emulate exactly what he or she has done and shortcut your way to success. This is applicable to both people you associate with on a daily basis and to choosing mentors to speed your journey.

> "If you want to be successful,
> Find someone who has achieved the results you want
> And copy what they do
> And you'll achieve the same results".
> **Tony Robbins**.

Women may share a lot of things (the blogosphere explosion is a testament to this) but having a strong mentor usually is not one, men seem to be more apt at networking with purpose and connecting with people who can help them rather than just sharing experiences.

Having a mentor is one the most critical factors for continuous growth and accelerated success. Picking both men and women mentors that tell you not what you want to hear but what you need to hear is priceless: men will give you an insight in the way things are (if we are to believe the "old boys club" exists) and they can be an inside ally and advocate. Women can guide you on potential obstacles they faced specifically as female and how they dealt with them.

Action point

I'm not going to make assumptions so I'm going to ask you outright: do you have a mentor (or hopefully more)?

If not, why not? If yes, how have they helped you so far?

....
....
....
....
....
....
....
....
....
....
....

Thinking about the new characteristics you are trying to gain: what other/additional mentors might you need in the future? Ideally you should look for people who have the qualities/skills/attitudes that you are trying to "fake" in spade — they should be evident in everything they do.

(If you have already someone, don't feel like you are being disloyal — it is not just OK to have different mentors for different things, it is highly recommended).

....
....
....
....
....
....
....
....
....
....
....

What are the professional associations in your field/sector that you can join to both up-skill yourself and network? List at list five possible organizations.

....
....
....
....
....
....
....
....
....
....
....
....
....
....

Now it is time to look for networking opportunities to meet your new mentors and level up. Look up at least at two events per week for the next three months

....
....
....
....
....
....
....
....
....
....
....
....
....
....

Now, think of specific examples of support/guidance that you need from your new mentor/s that would fulfill your need of "faking it".

....
....
....
....
....
....
....
....
....
....
....
....
....
....
....
....
....
....
....
....
....
....
....
....
....
....
....
....
....
....
....

3 things to be thankful for

Think back at the topic covered today — what are the 3 things you are grateful for, despite everything? Remember, if you can't think of any — you are not looking hard enough. Think again.

....
....
....
....
....
....
....
....
....
....
....
....
....
....
....
....
....
....
....
....
....
....
....
....
....

DAY 79: THINK OUTSIDE THE BOX:
WHAT BOX? ACT THE PART

The Monkey Mind/dump the c*** exercise

P **rompt:**
   Modeling

....
....
....
....
....
....
....
....
....
....
....
....
....
....

Mirror Mirror

Mirror, Mirror refers to the NeuroLinguistic Programming technique of Mirroring and Matching to build rapport.

Mirroring is one of the most useful NLP techniques there are, is innate and even chimps use mirroring within their groups.

It is useful to determine whether people are visual, audial, or kinaesthetic (you do so by listening to their language patterns) and consequently adapt your presentation and communication/language style to suit the specific audience and have more impact.

State	Primary sense	Language patterns
Visual	Sight	I see; it looks good
Audial	Hearing	Sounds good; that rings a bell
Kinaesthetic	Feeling	That doesn't feel right; I can't put my finger on it

Mimicking people who display the required skill sets and behavior, even if you worry about appearing like a fraud is very helpful, according to research.

Professor of organizational behavior Herminia Ibarra wrote in the *Harvard Business Review* about such (her) research "By viewing ourselves as works in progress, we multiply our capacity to learn, avoid being pigeonholed, and ultimately become better leaders. We're never too experienced to fake it till we learn it".

• • •

Action point

Look back at the exercises you have done so far: what are the language patterns that you have used primarily throughout?

....
....
....
....
....
....
....
....
....
....
....
....
....

What those language patterns correspond to: Visual, Audial or Kinaesthetic? Is that what you thought, believed you were?

....
....
....
....
....
....
....
....
....
....
....
....

Mirror and Match practice = look at the mentors you have chosen that display the required characteristics (that you do not possess) identified as needed to move you forward. Start to Mirror and Match (be careful not to come across as parroting).

It would be useful to start with people that have the same language patterns you have (e.g., Visual/Audial/Kinaesthetic) — this will make it much easier and look much.

....
....
....
....
....
....
....
....
....
....
....

Plan situations when you can carefully observe how they "act the part" (the characteristics) and how they project themselves (with the language patterns). Schedule.

....
....
....
....
....
....
....
....
....
....

Mirror and Match practice = now look around and identify three other people that display the aforementioned characteristics but this time choose people that have the other two language patterns. Same "qualities/behaviors" but different ways of expressing; this will expand your tool kit.

....
....
....
....
....
....
....
....
....
....
....
....
....
....
....

As previously, plan situations and schedule them.

....
....
....
....
....
....
....
....
....
....
....
....
....

3 things to be thankful for

Think back at the topic covered today — what are the 3 things you are grateful for, despite everything? Remember, if you can't think of any — you are not looking hard enough. Think again.

....
....
....
....
....
....
....
....
....
....
....
....
....
....
....
....
....
....
....
....
....
....
....
....
....

DAY 80: THINK OUTSIDE THE BOX: WHAT BOX? ACT THE PART

The Monkey Mind/dump the c*** exercise

Prompt:
    Act outside the box

....
....
....
....
....
....
....
....
....
....
....
....
....
....

Review time

Action point

By now you should have a clear view of your fears and root cause/s, your own personal barriers and definition of success, together with your what and why, know the price and decided to go for it plus three characteristics that you currently do not possess that you need to practice on.

Time to link them up...

....
....
....
....
....
....
....
....
....
....
....
....
....
....
....
....
....
....
....
....
....
....
....
....
....

3 things to be thankful for

Think back at the topic covered today — what are the 3 things you are grateful for, despite everything? Remember, if you can't think of any — you are not looking hard enough. Think again.

....
....
....
....
....
....
....
....
....
....
....
....
....
....
....
....
....
....
....
....
....
....
....
....
....

DAY 81 : REST, RELAXATION AND SOME REFLECTION

The Monkey Mind/dump the c*** exercise

P rompt:
Being judged

....
....
....
....
....
....
....
....
....
....
....
....
....
....

This page is intentionally left blank

3 things to be thankful for

Think back at the topic covered today — what are the 3 things you are grateful for, despite everything? Remember, if you can't think of any — you are not looking hard enough. Think again.

....
....
....
....
....
....
....
....
....
....
....
....
....
....
....
....
....
....
....
....
....
....
....
....
....
....
....

DAY 82 : REST, RELAXATION AND SOME REFLECTION

The Monkey Mind/dump the c*** exercise

P rompt:
Failure

....
....
....
....
....
....
....
....
....
....
....
....
....
....

This page is intentionally left blank

3 things to be thankful for

Think back at the topic covered today — what are the 3 things you are grateful for, despite everything? Remember, if you can't think of any — you are not looking hard enough. Think again.

....

....

....

....

....

....

....

....

....

....

....

....

....

....

....

....

....

....

....

....

....

....

....

....

DAY 83: THINK OUTSIDE THE BOX:
WHAT BOX? ACT THE PART

*The Monkey Mind/dump the c*** exercise*

P rompt:
Challenge

....
....
....
....
....
....
....
....
....
....
....
....
....
....

Change is inevitable. Progress is a choice: challenge 1

> *"Challenge yourself; it's the only path*
> *which leads to growth,"*
> **- Morgan Freeman.**

The time has now come to go for it full on and practice the "Fake it till you make it" philosophy.

This week I will present you with one challenge each day to push your boundaries and getting you out of your comfort zone and practicing a bit more "acting" up.

Ready?

Ok, here we go...

Today we are going to tackle dealing and adapting to change, getting your mind (and your body) down a different path.

Beginning with small changes that do not represent a real threat, such as eating, drinking, sleeping, dressing and so on. The idea is to place yourself in new arenas where you control the interactions and practice doing things differently

Challenge 1

Make a list of the twenty things you do every day, your routines from what you do in the morning, what side of the bed you sleep in, the way you comb your hair , etc., etc. (I think you get the drift here...) to your evening routine.

Once you list them all, proceed to do something different for each and every one. If you drink coffee everyday, try tea (or chocolate or, God forbid, water!). If you sleep on the right hand side of the bed, try the left.

. . .

Make it a game; you don't have to like the new things you are trying. You don't have to think about them or philosophize either. Just go down the list and do something different for each item you have listed.

And if you want to be really adventurous, don't pick the safe choice as an alternative but use this opportunity to do something really uncomfortable.

Go.

....

....

....

....

....

....

....

....

....

....

....

....

....

....

....

....

....

....

....

....

....

....

....

....

....

....

....
....
....
....
....
....
....
....
....
....
....
....
....
....
....
....
....
....
....
....
....
....
....
....
....

"The hardest thing to do is leaving your comfort zone.
But you have to let go of the life you're familiar with and take the risk to live the
life you dream about,"
- T. Arigo.

3 things to be thankful for

Think back at the topic covered today — what are the 3 things you are grateful for, despite everything? Remember, if you can't think of any — you are not looking hard enough. Think again.

....
....
....
....
....
....
....
....
....
....
....
....
....
....
....
....
....
....
....
....
....
....
....
....
....
....
....

DAY 84: THINK OUTSIDE THE BOX: WHAT BOX? ACT THE PART

The Monkey Mind/dump the c*** exercise

P rompt:
Comfort zone

....
....
....
....
....
....
....
....
....
....
....
....
....
....

Change is inevitable. Progress is a choice: challenge 2

> *"The more failures, the more successes.*
> *Period"* - **Tom Peters.**

Challenge 2

Dare to be mediocre. Fail on purpose. Yes, that's right. Today try something new and make a mess of it. In front of people. ON PURPOSE.

Describe what is the worst thing that could possibly happen.

....

....

....

....

....

....

....

....

....

....

....

....

....

....

....

....

....

....

....

....

....

....

....

Done?

Now go ahead and do it anyway.

Go on, I'll wait ...

....
....
....
....
....
....
....
....
....
....
....
....
....
....

OK, how bad was it? Anybody died? Non? I thought so ...

> *"It is not failure itself that holds you back;*
> *it's the fear of failure that paralyzes you,"*
> **- Brian Tracy**

Things do not magically improve by themselves. You need to do something different. Act differently.

3 things to be thankful for

Think back at the topic covered today — what are the 3 things you are grateful for, despite everything? Remember, if you can't think of any — you are not looking hard enough. Think again.

....
....
....
....
....
....
....
....
....
....
....
....
....
....
....
....
....
....
....
....
....
....
....
....
....
....

DAY 85: THINK OUTSIDE THE BOX: WHAT BOX? ACT THE PART

The Monkey Mind/dump the c*** exercise

P **rompt:**
  What's the worst that can happen?

....
....
....
....
....
....
....
....
....
....
....
....
....

Change is inevitable. Progress is a choice: challenge 3

Say YES.

Saying yes means be surprised at what is possible and what you are actually capable of doing. Means being open and taking risks, and trying over and over until you actually succeed.

So say yes, and then figure out how to do it, learn and fail fast. And when you do that, you are the one in charge.

"If someone offers you a great opportunity but you are not sure you can do it, say yes — then learn how to do it later." - **Richard Branson.**

Challenge 3

Start saying yes right now. Wake up and say, yes. Say yes to a project that is totally new for you and out of your comfort zone. And then over deliver. Today, start saying yes to a personal challenge .

....
....
....
....
....
....
....
....
....
....
....
....
....
....
....
....
....

....
....
....
....
....
....
....
....
....
....
....
....
....
....
....
....
....
....
....
....
....
....
....
....
....
....
....
....
....
....
....
....
....

The more you say yes, the easier it becomes.

3 things to be thankful for

Think back at the topic covered today — what are the 3 things you are grateful for, despite everything? Remember, if you can't think of any — you are not looking hard enough. Think again.

....
....
....
....
....
....
....
....
....
....
....
....
....
....
....
....
....
....
....
....
....
....
....
....
....
....
....

DAY 86: THINK OUTSIDE THE BOX: WHAT BOX? ACT THE PART

The Monkey Mind/dump the c*** exercise

P **rompt:**
     What's the best that can happen?

....
....
....
....
....
....
....
....
....
....
....
....
....
....

Change is inevitable. Progress is a choice: challenge 4

Say YES some more.

Richard Branson is a great fan of saying yes (apparently so much so, that he's nicknamed: "Dr Yes," among his Virgin employees). He says it's better to say yes instead of no because "opportunity favors the bold — this is a lesson that I learned early on, and have used to guide the Virgin story."

Challenge 4

Today say yes to a business challenge — even better: volunteer. Ask yourself for a change: what is the best that could happen?

....
....
....
....
....
....
....
....
....
....
....
....
....
....
....
....
....
....
....
....
....

....
....
....
....
....
....
....
....
....
....
....
....
....
....
....
....
....
....
....
....
....
....
....
....
....
....
....
....
....
....

The more you say yes, the easier it becomes. And the more confident you become. When you keep saying yes in business, people will be attracted to you and give you more and more opportunities.

3 things to be thankful for

Think back at the topic covered today — what are the 3 things you are grateful for, despite everything? Remember, if you can't think of any — you are not looking hard enough. Think again.

....
....
....
....
....
....
....
....
....
....
....
....
....
....
....
....
....
....
....
....
....
....
....
....
....

DAY 87: THINK OUTSIDE THE BOX: WHAT BOX? ACT THE PART

The Monkey Mind/dump the c*** exercise

P**rompt:**
    "May the odds always be in your favor".

....

....

....

....

....

....

....

....

....

....

....

....

....

....

Change is inevitable. Progress is a choice: challenge 5

Say yes, more and more ...

> *"Probably some of the best things that have ever happened to you in life,*
> *happened because you said yes to something.*
> *Otherwise things just sort of stay the same,"*
> **– Danny Wallace.**

Challenge 5

Today say yes to act, for the full day, like the person who has that fancy position you want. See yourself as that person. How would she talk? How would she behave?

Act as if.

....
....
....
....
....
....
....
....
....
....
....
....
....
....
....
....
....
....

....
....
....
....
....
....
....
....
....
....
....
....
....
....
....
....
....
....
....
....
....
....
....
....
....
....
....
....

"Do the one thing you think you cannot do.
Fail at it. Try again. Do better the second time.
The only people who never tumble are those who
never mount the high wire"
— Oprah Winfrey.

3 things to be thankful for

Think back at the topic covered today — what are the 3 things you are grateful for, despite everything? Remember, if you can't think of any — you are not looking hard enough. Think again.

....
....
....
....
....
....
....
....
....
....
....
....
....
....
....
....
....
....
....
....
....
....
....
....
....

DAY 88 : REST, RELAXATION AND SOME REFLECTION

*The Monkey Mind/dump the c*** exercise*

P rompt:
Self-belief

....
....
....
....
....
....
....
....
....
....
....
....
....

This page is intentionally left blank

3 things to be thankful for

Think back at the topic covered today — what are the 3 things you are grateful for, despite everything? Remember, if you can't think of any — you are not looking hard enough. Think again.

....
....
....
....
....
....
....
....
....
....
....
....
....
....
....
....
....
....
....
....
....
....
....
....
....

DAY 89 : REST, RELAXATION AND SOME REFLECTION

*The Monkey Mind/dump the c*** exercise*

P rompt:
Empowerment

....
....
....
....
....
....
....
....
....
....
....
....
....
....

This page is intentionally left blank

3 things to be thankful for

Think back at the topic covered today — what are the 3 things you are grateful for, despite everything? Remember, if you can't think of any — you are not looking hard enough. Think again.

....
....
....
....
....
....
....
....
....
....
....
....
....
....
....
....
....
....
....
....
....
....
....
....
....

DAY 90 : ALL TOGETHER NOW

The Monkey Mind/dump the c*** exercise

P rompt:
Future

....
....
....
....
....
....
....
....
....
....
....
....
....
....

All together now

Now is the time to look back at the journey for the past 30 days, make some decisions and plan your way forward.

Action point

Describe your journey for the last 30 days — the good, the bad and the ugly.

....
....
....
....
....
....
....
....
....
....
....
....
....
....
....
....

What was the lowest point and why?

....
....
....
....
....
....
....
....

What was the highest point and why?

....
....
....
....
....
....
....
....
....
....

What have you learned about yourself?

....
....
....
....
....
....
....
....
....

What do you really (REALLY) want to achieve — the ultimate goal?

....
....
....
....
....
....
....
....
....
....

Why do you want it? What will give you?

....
....
....
....
....
....
....
....
....
....
....
....

What is your definition of success?

....
....
....
....
....
....
....
....

What price, if any, are you willing to pay?

....
....
....
....
....
....
....
....

What are the barriers you are facing to achieve your goal and how are you going to tackle them now?

....
....
....
....
....
....
....
....
....
....

Career mapping: your next role toward the ultimate goal (if not the same).

....
....
....
....
....
....
....
....
....

List the characteristics/qualities/skills you currently do not possess that you've identified as needed to achieve your career goal/s.

....
....
....
....
....
....
....

Describe the type of role models/mentor you need to support you in gaining the characteristics/qualities/skills and the steps you are going to take to start the mentor/mentee relationship.

....
....
....
....
....
....
....
....
....
....
....

Plan and schedule appropriate occasions for you to start practicing to Mirror and Match (Visual, Audial and Kinaesthetic).

....
....
....
....
....
....
....
....

Now reflect on what you have learned from challenging yourself.

....
....
....
....
....
....

Which challenge was the easiest? Why so — be specific.

....
....
....
....
....
....
....
....
....

Which challenge was the hardest? What did you find particularly difficult? Be specific.

....
....
....
....
....
....
....
....
....

How did you overcome the difficulty?

....
....
....
....
....
....
....

Now, plan challenges to "act the part" for the next four weeks :

Week 1

....
....
....
....
....
....

Week 2

....
....
....
....
....
....

Week 3

....
....
....
....
....
....

Week 4

....
....
....
....
....

3 things to be thankful for

Think back at the topic covered today — what are the 3 things you are grateful for, despite everything? Remember, if you can't think of any — you are not looking hard enough. Think again.

....
....
....
....
....
....
....
....
....
....
....
....
....
....
....
....
....
....
....
....
....
....
....
....

ONE LAST THING

You have made through the book, phew …
Thanks for reading it all and working through ALL the exercises! You did, right? :-)

Now it's when the real work begins, if you quit now, you will miss the best part of your hero journey, the real adventure.

I would suggest at this point that you form a group of some kind, a protective professional circle, some partners in crime.

Find and connect with people who are already there, asking questions on their decision-making process — what, why, how they make decisions, critical paths.

Share stories.

Get inspired and inspire.

"You are the average of the 5 people you surround yourself with" – **Napoleon Hill**.

More than anything, remember these three things:

1. Perfection does not exist, Be awesome instead
2. Anything is possible
3. We are all in this together: if we can take care of one another, appreciate each other, we all gain — women inspiring and empowering other women.

And when you start making excuses and blame someone remember:

STOP IT!
It is all in
your head
#SmashYourCeiling

KEY DATES IN INTERNATIONAL WOMEN HISTORY

FROM THE UNITED NATIONS FOUNDATION

1911 First ever International Women's Day celebrated.

1913 Marie Curie is awarded the Nobel Prize for Chemistry. Norwegian women gain the right to vote.

1915 Women from the US and Europe gather in The Hague in the Netherlands for the first International Congress of Women – later known as the Women's International League for Peace and Freedom.

1916 Jeannette Rankin of Montana is the first woman elected to the US Congress.

1918 Women in Russia strike for "bread and peace." The strike helps initiate the revolution that results in the overthrow of the imperial government. March 8, the day the strike began, is later chosen to mark International Women's Day.
Canadian women gain the right to vote.
British women over 30 are granted the right to vote.
The Indian National Congress supports giving women the right to vote. Hungarian feminist Rosika Schwimmer is appointed ambassador to Switzerland.

1919 Women enter the British House of Commons for the first time with Lady Astor's appointment.

1920 The XIX Amendment to the US Constitution, giving women the right to vote, becomes law when it is ratified by two-thirds of the states.

The League of Women Voters is founded.

The Treaty of Versailles states that women must receive equal pay as their male counterparts.

1922 The National Council of Women is created in Chile to fight for women's rights.

The Brazilian Federation for the Advancement of Women is founded by Bertha Lutz.

1923 Family planning pioneer Margaret Sanger opens the first legal, physician-run birth control clinic in the United States.

1925 Nellie Tayloe Ross is the first woman governor of a US State (Wyoming).

1926 Gertrude Ederle is the first woman to swim the English Channel.

1928 Women compete for the first time in Olympic field events.

1931 Activist Jane Addams received the Nobel Prize for Peace. She is the first American woman to win a Nobel Peace Prize.

Gertrude Vanderbilt Whitney founded The Whitney Museum of American Art in New York City, becoming the first woman to found a major art museum.

1932 Amelia Earhart makes the first solo flight by a woman across the Atlantic. She is the first woman to be awarded the Distinguished Flying Cross.

Alexandra Kollontai is appointed ambassador from the Soviet Union to Sweden. She is considered the first woman ambassador in modern history.

1933 Frances Perkins is appointed Secretary of Labor by Franklin D. Roosevelt. She is the first woman appointed to a cabinet position in the American government.

1934 Women in Brazil and Thailand gained the right to vote.

1937 Cuba requires equal pay for equal work regardless of gender.

1945 Eleanor Roosevelt becomes the American delegate for the recently formed United Nations. In 1946 she was elected as the head of the United Nations Human Rights Commission. She is instrumental in drafting the Declaration of Human Rights.

1946 The United Nations Commission on the Status of Women is formed.
  The Sudanese Women's League is founded. It is modern Sudan's first women's organization.
  Women in the Philippines gain the right to vote.

1948 In Japan, women vote and run for election in the House of Representatives for the first time.

1949 Women gain the right to vote in Israel and South Korea.
  The Peronista Feminist Party is founded in Argentinian by Eva Perón.
  The Second Sex (Le Deuxième Sexe), by French feminist Simone de Beauvoir, is published. It has a major impact on understanding of gender.

1952 Molecular biologist Rosalind Franklin begins work at King's College, London. She goes on to play a major role in the discovery of DNA.
  Israel passes the Women's Equal Rights Act, making gender discrimination illegal.

1954 Colombian women are granted the right to vote.

1955 Rosa Park's refusal to give up her seat to a white man on a bus, and her subsequent arrest, is used to launch the Montgomery bus boycott.

1956 In Israel, Golda Meir is appointed Minister of Foreign Affairs. She is the only woman in the Israeli cabinet.

1958 Swedish diplomat Agda Rössel is the first woman to head a permanent delegation to the United Nations.

1960 Sirimavo Bandaranaike is elected as Prime Minister of Sri Lanka.

In Japan, Nakayama Masa is appointed Minister of Health and Welfare. She is Japan's first female cabinet member.

1961 Paraguay grants women the right to vote. It is the last republic in the Americas to do so.

1963 Betty Friedan published The Feminine Mystique, which galvanizes the women's rights movement.

Valentina Tereshkova of Russia becomes the first woman in space.

Iranian women gain the right to vote.

1964 Title VII of the Civil Rights Act prohibits discrimination in employment on the basis of race or sex.

1965 The Supreme Court ruling in the Griswold v. State of Connecticut case states that laws prohibiting the use of birth control are unconstitutional.

1966 The National Organization of Women is founded by feminist Betty Friedan and other delegates to the Third National Conference of the Commission on the Status of Women.

Indira Gandhi becomes India's first female Prime Minister.

1968 Soong Ching-ling is named Co Chairwoman of the People's Republic of China. She is the first non-royal woman to lead the state of China.

1969 Golda Meir becomes Israel's first female prime minister.

1970 The Boston Women's Health Book Collective helps launch the women's health movement in the US by publishing Our Bodies, Ourselves.

1971 India launched its National Commission on the Status of Women.

Helga Pederson becomes the first female judge on the European Court of Human Rights.

Women in Switzerland gain the right to vote.

1972 Title IX of the Education Amendments bans sex discrimination in schools. Enrollment of women in athletics programs and professional schools increases dramatically.

Ms Magazine is launched by a group of feminists, including Gloria Steinem, as an outlet for feminist voices in America.

1973 Tennis star Billie Jean King wins the "battle-of-the-sexes" tennis match against Bobby Riggs. The event is highly publicized and serves as inspiration for demands for equal rights and opportunities for female athletes.

The Roe v. Wade decision by the Supreme Court rules that a woman has a constitutional right to abortion.

Sex segregated "help wanted" ads are banned following the Supreme Court ruling in Pittsburgh Press v. Pittsburgh Commission on Human Relations, 413 US 376. Women in Jordan, gain the right to vote.

1974 Maria Estela (Isabela) Martinez de Peron becomes the first woman to lead an American nation when she succeeds her husband as President of Argentina. She is also the first female president of Argentina.

1975 The UN names 1975 International Women's Year. March 8 has been celebrated as International Women's Day ever since.

The World Congress for International Women's Year opens in Berlin. The first World Conference on Women is held in Mexico City.

The Pregnancy and Discrimination Act is passed to prohibit discrimination on the basis of pregnancy, childbirth, or related medical conditions.

1976 1976 – 1985 The United Nations' Decade for Women.

Tina Anselmi becomes the first woman in the Italian cabinet when she is appointed Labour minister.

1977 Discrimination on the basis of sex or marital status is prohibited by law in Canada.

Nigerian women gain the right to vote.

1978 Women's History Week is first celebrated in Sonoma County, California. Kuwaiti women's protests successfully keep a proposed law prohibiting women from work in offices from legally passing.

1979 The UN General Assembly adopts the Convention on the Eliminations of All Forms of Discrimination again Women. It defines what counts as discrimination again women and creates an agenda for nations to adopt.

Mother Teresa is awarded the Nobel Peace Prize for her work in the slums of Calcutta, India.

Maria de Lourdes Pintasilgo became the first female Prime Minister of Portugal.

Lidia Geiler is elected President of Bolivia. She is the first woman to hold this position.

Margaret Thatcher becomes Great Britain's first female Prime Minister.

Simone Weil of France becomes the first woman elected President of the European Parliament.

Nigerian women gain the right to vote.

1980 Vigdis Finnbogadottir becomes the first woman elected President of Iceland.

1981 Jeanne Kirkpatrick becomes the first female US ambassador to the United Nations.

Sandra Day O'Connor is the first woman on the US Supreme Court, serving until 2006.

Gro Harlem Brundtland becomes the first woman Prime Minister of Norway.

1982 Agatha Barbara is the first woman elected President of Malta. Milka Planinc is the first woman to become Prime Minister of Yugoslavia.

1983 Sally Ride becomes the first American woman to travel in space.

1985 Eugenia Charles is the first woman to become Prime Minister in the Caribbean.

1986 Corazon Aquino is the first woman to be elected president of the Philippines.

Maria Liberia-Peters becomes the first woman Prime Minister of the Netherlands Antilles.

1987 Congress expands Women's History Week to a month-long event celebrated in March.

Wilma Mankiller is named the first woman Chief of the Cherokee Nation. She is the first woman to lead a major Native American Tribe in modern history.

1988 Benazir Bhutto is the first woman to lead a Muslim country in modern history when she becomes prime minister of Pakistan.

1990 Mary Robinson is the first female President of Ireland.

Ertha Pascal-Trouillot is the first woman to be elected President of Haiti.

Carmen Lawrence is the first female Premier of Australia.

1991 Edith Cresson is the first woman Prime Minister of France.

Khaleda Zia Rahman is the first woman Prime Minister of Bangladesh.

1992 Rita Johnston is the first female Premier of Canada.

Hanna Suchocka is the first female Prime Minister of Poland.

1993 Janet Reno is the first woman Attorney General of the United States.

Toni Morrison becomes the first African American woman to win the Nobel Prize for literature.

Sylvie Kinigi is the first female Prime Minister of Burundi.

Tansu Ciller is Turkey's first female Prime Minister.

1995 The International Conference on Population and Development in Cairo creates a Program of Action. Some of the goals outlined by the Program of Action include, achieving universal education, reducing infant and child mortality, reducing maternal mortality, and achieving access to reproductive and sexual health services including family planning.

The 4th World Conference on Women is held in Beijing, China.

1997 Madeleine Albright is sworn in as the first woman US Secretary of State.

Jenny Shipley becomes the first woman Prime Minister of New Zealand.

1999 Mireya Moscoso is elected as Panama's first female president. She oversees the US handover of the Panama Canal.

2000 The Millennium Development Goals (MDGs) are developed to improve the conditions of the world's poorest countries by year 2015. The goals are to:

1. Eradicate extreme poverty and hunger
2. Achieve universal primary
3. Promote gender equality
4. Reduce child mortality
5. Improve maternal mortality
6. Combat HIV / AIDS, Malaria and other diseases
7. Ensure environmental sustainability and
8. Create global partnerships for development.

Beverley McLachlin becomes the first female Chief Justice of the Supreme Court of Canada.

The Canadian Supreme Court had ruled that women were not "persons" 70 years earlier.

Tarja Halonen is elected Finland's first woman president.

2001 A referendum including the right of women to stand for office is approved by voters in Bahrain.

2004 Megawati Sukarnoputri becomes the first female President of the Republic of Indonesia.

2005 Condoleezza Rice is the first African American woman to serve as US Secretary of State.

2004 Wangari Maathai, a Kenyan environmental activist, is awarded the Nobel Peace Prize. She is the first black African woman to win a Nobel Prize.

Kuwaiti women gain the right to vote.

2006 Ellen Johnson Sirleaf becomes the first female President in Africa when she is elected in Liberia.

Michelle Bachelet is the first woman elected President of Chile.

2007 Nancy Pelosi is sworn in as the first female Speaker of the US House of Representatives, one of the most powerful posts in the US government.

2008 Pratibha Patil is elected as the first woman President of India. The first all female UN Peacekeeping unit is deployed. It is made up of over 100 police women from Indian and it is sent to Liberia.

2009 Michelle Obama becomes the first African-American First Lady of the United States.

Sonia Sotomayor becomes the first Hispanic, and third woman, to serve as a justice of the US Supreme Court.

2011 UN Women is formed out of a number of existing UN organizations. UN Women is formed to further the empowerment of women and girls and to advocate for gender equality.

2013 Malala Yousafzai delivers the memorable speech "Education For All" at the United Nation, in her first public appearance on her 16th birthday in 2013 after surviving a gunshot wound.

20 -- Write your name: what will be your legacy?

(This page was left blank intentionally).

AUTHOR'S NOTE

Thank you so much for reading and working through *90 Days to Reboot Your Career*.

I hope you enjoyed this book and it has challenged, perhaps overthrown some of your negative beliefs about yourself and, most importantly, has spurred you into taking control over your own narrative, your career and, ultimately, over your life.

A review would be much appreciated as it helps other readers discover the story. Thanks.

If you sign up for my newsletter you'll be notified of give-aways, new releases and receive personal updates from behind the scenes of my business and books.

Go to www.thepeoplealchemist.com to get started.

Bibliography

I read a lot of books as part of my research. Some of them together with other references include:

Write For Your Life - **Lawrence Block**
The Artist Way - **Julia Cameron**
Tools of Titans - **Tim Ferriss**
Psycho-Cybernetics - **Maxwell Maltz**
Self Mastery Through Conscious Autosuggestion - **Émile Coué**

ALSO BY LAURA MARIANI

<u>Fiction</u>

The Nine Lives of Gabrielle: For Three She Plays Trilogy out 23 April 2022

Gabrielle, from the diary of (The Nine Lives of Gabrielle #1)

A vivid portrait of one day in a woman's life through her morning pages. The city of London during lockdown the background.

<u>Non-Fiction</u>

STOP IT! It is all in your head

The RULE BOOK to Smash The infamous glass ceiling - For women & young women everywhere — personal transformation & success 101.

The Think, Look & Act The Part Series.

Think The Part

Upgrade your consciousness and mind-set. Make winning a key part

of your life and business.

Look The Part

Upgrade your personal brand. Make presenting your unique Best Self a key part of your life and business.

Act The Part

A personal coach to act in spite of fear, right here, right now.

Keep an eye for new releases, giveaways and pre-release specials by checking at www.thepeoplealchemist.com

You can also buy books and courses directly from the author at www. payhip.com/LauraMariani

#THEWOMANALCHEMIST TOOLBOX

Resources and products to help #TheWomanAlchemist in every woman to change her life/career and transmute any circumstance into gold. Here are some of the tools available.

Planners

2021-2026 5 year Planner for Women In Business

2021 - 2026 5 Year Planner for Female Entrepreneurs

Journals

The Monkey Mind/Dump The C**p on a page Journal

Freewriting for Business: Dump The C**p on a page and Level Up Your Career Journal

Freewriting for Business: Dump The C**p on a page and Exercise Your Creativity

Gratitude Journal: Your Own Portable Book of Magic

Gratitude Journal for Women In Business: Unlock Ignite Transform Your Career with Gratitude #SmashYourCeiling

Gratitude Journal For Female Entrepreneurs:Unlock Ignite Transform Your Business with Gratitude

Notebooks

I Think It I Write It Happens Notebook

I Think It I Write It I Grow It Notebook

I Think It I Write It I Create It Notebook

ACKNOWLEDGMENTS

Special thanks to the amazing Women Alchemists, as I call them, that so kindly agreed to be interviewed and share their story.

In no particular order – Natasha Makhijani, Rachel Dipper, Jackie Smithen, Emmajane Taylor-Moran, Karen Green, Liz Ward, Ela Slutski & Galit Bauer, Elena Kale, Katie Owen, Sophie Thorne, Alexandra Wall, Julie Bishop, Kirsten Rees, Cheryl Luzet, Irina Bragin, Rachel Carrell, Claire Curzon, Sally Bunkham, Yasmin Vorajee, Ute Amann-Seidel , Anne-Sophie Whitehead, Jacqui Burge, Anna Cousins.

Printed in Great Britain
by Amazon